The Cambridge Introduction to
J. M. Coetzee

The South African novelist and Nobel Laureate J. M. Coetzee is
widely studied around the world and attracts considerable critical
attention. With the publication of *Disgrace* Coetzee began to
enjoy popular as well as critical acclaim, but his work can be as
challenging as it is impressive. This book is addressed to students
and readers of Coetzee: it is an up-to-date survey of the writer's
fiction and context, written accessibly for those new to his work.
All of the fiction is discussed, and the brooding presence of the
political situation in South Africa, during the first part of his
career, is given serious attention in a comprehensive account of
the author's main influences. The revealing strand of confessional
writing in the latter half of Coetzee's career is given full
consideration. This introduction will help new readers
understand and appreciate one of the most important and
challenging authors in contemporary literature.

Dominic Head is Professor of Modern English Literature at the
University of Nottingham. His many publications include *The
Cambridge Introduction to Modern British Fiction, 1950–2000*
(Cambridge, 2002) and (as editor) *The Cambridge Guide to
Literature in English*, third edition (Cambridge, 2006).

The Cambridge Introduction to
J. M. Coetzee

DOMINIC HEAD

CAMBRIDGE
UNIVERSITY PRESS

CAMBRIDGE UNIVERSITY PRESS

Cambridge, New York, Melbourne, Madrid, Cape Town, Singapore, São Paulo, Delhi

Cambridge University Press
The Edinburgh Building, Cambridge CB2 8RU, UK

Published in the United States of America by Cambridge University Press, New York

www.cambridge.org
Information on this title: www.cambridge.org/9780521687096

First published 2009

Printed in the United Kingdom at the University Press, Cambridge

A catalogue record for this publication is available from the British Library

Library of Congress Cataloguing in Publication data
Head, Dominic.
 The Cambridge introduction to J. M. Coetzee / Dominic Head.
  p. cm. – (Cambridge introductions to literature)
 Includes bibliographical references and index.
 ISBN 978-0-521-86747-4 – ISBN 978-0-521-68709-6 (pbk.)
 1. Coetzee, J. M., 1940 – Criticism and interpretation. I. Title. II. Series.
 PR9369.3.C58Z675 2009
 823′.914–dc22   2009000060

ISBN 978-0-521-86747-4 hardback
ISBN 978-0-521-68709-6 paperback

Contents

Abbreviations

AI	*Age of Iron.* 1990; Harmondsworth: Penguin, 1991
B	*Boyhood: Scenes From Provincial Life.* London: Secker and Warburg, 1997
D	*Dusklands.* 1974; Harmondsworth: Penguin, 1983
DBY	*Diary of a Bad Year.* London: Harvill Secker, 2007
Dis	*Disgrace.* London: Secker and Warburg, 1999
DP	*Doubling the Point: Essays and Interviews,* ed. David Attwell. Cambridge, MA: Harvard University Press, 1992
EC	*Elizabeth Costello: Eight Lessons.* London: Secker and Warburg, 2003
F	*Foe.* 1986; Harmondsworth: Penguin, 1987
GO	*Giving Offense: Essays on Censorship.* Chicago: University of Chicago Press, 1996
IHC	*In the Heart of the Country.* 1977; Harmondsworth: Penguin, 1982
LA	*The Lives of Animals,* ed. Amy Gutman. Princeton: Princeton University Press, 1999
MK	*Life and Times of Michael K.* 1983; Harmondsworth: Penguin, 1985
MP	*The Master of Petersburg.* London: Secker and Warburg, 1994
SM	*Slow Man.* London: Secker and Warburg, 2005
WB	*Waiting for the Barbarians.* 1980; Harmondsworth: Penguin, 1982
WW	*White Writing: On the Culture of Letters in South Africa.* New Haven: Yale University Press, 1988
Y	*Youth.* London: Secker and Warburg, 2002

Preface

The South African novelist J. M. Coetzee is one of the most highly respected – and most frequently studied – contemporary authors. His novels occupy a special place in South African literature, and in the development of the twentieth- and 21st-century novel more generally. They are widely taught, internationally, on undergraduate modules, and interest amongst postgraduate students is high. He was the first novelist to win the Booker Prize twice (for *Life and Times of Michael K* in 1983, and *Disgrace* in 1999), and has been awarded the Nobel Prize for Literature (2003). With the publication of *Disgrace* Coetzee began to enjoy popular as well as critical acclaim. Nevertheless, he is a difficult writer who engages with complex ideas, and it is the task of this book to explain the significance of Coetzee in an introductory spirit. This is a challenge, because his works can make an instant and impressive impact on readers, who are then sometimes uncertain as to how to understand, or account for that impact.

It is sometimes said that postmodernism arrived in Africa with the publication, in 1974, of *Dusklands*, Coetzee's first novel (although he is frequently discussed as a 'late modernist'). Presented as a pair of linked novellas, *Dusklands* associates its portrayal of eighteenth-century Dutch imperialism in South Africa with an anatomy of the terror that underpins US policy in Vietnam. These juxtaposed and bleak psychological fictions constitute an early instance of the contemporary 'internationalization' of the novel; and they raise questions that have become central to the academic study of the novel: how does literary writing bear upon critical definitions of modernism/ postmodernism and colonialism/postcolonialism? How can 'history' be imagined in novels? As Coetzee's literary career has unfolded, in tandem with a distinguished academic career, his creative writing has repeatedly pushed at the questions that have been central to his life and times: what does it mean when an author pledges allegiance to the discourse of fiction (rather than the discourse of politics)? Is there a function for a literary canon? And what kind of ethical stance can be claimed for the novel, and by the academic-novelist?

It should also be acknowledged that Coetzee is an accomplished essayist. His essays, written in a customary lucid and elegant style, cover a range of important contemporary debates, including: the modernist legacy; colonial identity; and the question of censorship. This book is principally concerned with Coetzee the novelist, so there is no extended discussion of the non-fiction in its own right. Reference is made to the essays, however, where they illuminate aspects of Coetzee's fiction.

For the first part of his career, up to and including the publication of *Age of Iron* (1990), it was inevitable that Coetzee's writing would be received as a response – usually, though not always, an oblique response – to the era of apartheid in South Africa. Coetzee occupied an interim position in a very particular branch of postcolonial writing: the literature of the 'post-colonizer'. This transitional site between Europe and Africa can be articulated by appropriating Coetzee's own comment on selected pre-apartheid writers of the 1920s and 1930s: 'white writing is white only in so far as it is generated by the concerns of people no longer European, not yet African' (*WW*, p. 11). That implication of a natural transition, as yet to come, carries its own censure of apartheid society where both biological and cultural hybridity were artificially policed and prevented.

There is also a broader colonial resonance in the theme of 'European ideas writing themselves out in Africa' (*DP*, pp. 338–9); but in Coetzee's work this has inevitably attracted censure from those impatient for political change in late- and then post-apartheid South Africa, who felt that the novelist had a duty to engage *overtly* with the world of history and politics. That sense of pressure in South African literary culture, to make writing serve a political purpose, has waned somewhat since the demise of apartheid and the democratic election of 1994. Yet Coetzee has continued to be a target of criticism where he has been perceived to be failing in his public 'duties'. Coetzee's writing – perhaps internalizing the sense of constraint in South African society – has been dominated by specifically literary questions, and does not produce the more obvious gestures of engagement and commitment that some commentators called for. (Coetzee's fellow South African novelist – and fellow Nobel Laureate – Nadine Gordimer, was one.) Yet Coetzee's apparently oblique engagements embody their own gesture of resistance, specifically a resistance to the idea that literature must supplement – and so be in thrall to – an agreed history 'out there'. Coetzee works on the principle that the novel should not supplement history, but establish a position of rivalry with it. This is one of the ways in which his emphasis on questions of textuality is a deployment of postmodernist (or late modernist) and post-structuralist concerns fitted to his context.

In his more recent phase of writing – and especially since the publication of *Disgrace* (1999), that groundbreaking second Booker winner – his concerns have reached a wider readership, in an exemplary instance of how the burning issues of professionalized academia can be made relevant to a non-academic audience. His readers can expect to be required to reflect on public morality and personal responsibility, the problems of the regulated society, mortality, and the function of the reader. As the shadow of apartheid recedes, so has Coetzee's writing struck out in vital new directions. His novels have all had a power and a resonance beyond the narrow concerns of academia, though this tendency to reach beyond the constraints of intellectual life has become more pronounced. For his entire output, however, the same critical problem obtains: how to treat the gap between the surface lucidity and the underlying complexity of Coetzee's work, how to indicate his intellectual importance without leaving the non-specialist behind. This book is an attempt to bridge that gap.

In a related sense, 'bridging' is one way of defining Coetzee's overall appeal and achievement. In the work preparatory to his book *The Lives of Animals* (1999), later incorporated in the novel *Elizabeth Costello* (2003), Coetzee gave a series of public lectures which were actually extracts from this fictional work-in-progress. One such was his Dawson Scott Memorial Lecture 'What is Realism?', given at the PEN International Writer's Day at London's Café Royal in 1996, which was finally to form the opening chapter of *Elizabeth Costello*. Presenting this piece of fiction as a lecture, which incorporates a fictionalized lecture also entitled 'What is Realism?', Coetzee struck upon a form of performance which simultaneously cultivated 'the realist illusion' while reflecting self-consciously upon it. This is the essence of Coetzee's 'bridging' – bringing together the concerns of academic and non-academic readers, in a mode that puts a heavy burden on the realist bridge upon which it still depends.

This is an astonishing duality, a mode of writing that combines a sophisticated control of fictional time and space with a self-consciousness that continually threatens to disrupt it, but without ever quite doing so. At its best, Coetzee's fiction generates a beguiling, elegiac yet brooding resonance. The result is a series of poetic and elusive novels which, like the characters they contain, wilfully resist any critical attempt to master or reduce. This means that the element of misrepresentation that is evident in all criticism is, perhaps, highlighted most especially in criticism of Coetzee's novels. And this may sound like a particular hostage to fortune at the beginning of an introductory volume of this kind; but it does give me the opportunity to place stress on the need for openness in the reading of a novel by Coetzee, even while acknowledging the acute difficulty of sustaining that openness.

The various elements of ambivalence that surround Coetzee's work – the implicit debate about representation, his sense of contextual constraint as a writer, and the cultivated elusiveness of the novels themselves – are suggestively caught in this remarkable statement by Coetzee from an interview with David Attwell, which I will leave unglossed. I hope it will resonate in the mind of the reader consulting the pages that follow:

> I am not a herald of community or anything else . . . I am someone who has intimations of freedom (as every chained prisoner has) and constructs representations – which are shadows themselves – of people slipping their chains and turning their faces to the light.   (*DP*, p. 341)

Chapter 1

Coetzee's life

Anyone familiar with Coetzee's novels knows that they are challenging, and elusive of interpretation. And what is true of the work is true of the author himself: Coetzee is a very private person, who has a reputation for being unforthcoming with interviewers. This means that the available details of Coetzee's life are sparse (and not truly verifiable). However, in a paradoxical move, he has begun a process in the latter half of his career of developing a complex form of confessional writing, in which autobiographical elements are prominent. The most obvious books, here, are the two memoirs, *Boyhood: Scenes from Provincial Life* (1997) and *Youth* (2002), the former covering some key formative experiences up to the age of thirteen, the latter pinpointing formative moments between 1959 and 1964, with an emphasis on Coetzee's experiences in London. These enrich our understanding of the author's life – or, at least his chosen self-projection – but they must also be treated with caution. As exercises in the confessional mode, they also invite reflection on this mode, and sometimes do so by encouraging the reader initially to accept at face value accounts which must then be re-evaluated. *Youth*, which was published as 'fiction', is particularly challenging in this regard.

John Maxwell Coetzee was born in Cape Town on 9 February 1940. His boyhood in the Cape Province was dominated by cultural conflicts, consequent upon his situation as an English-speaking white South African, and the social location of his schoolteacher mother, and his father, who practised intermittently as a lawyer. One interesting detail, with significance for Coetzee's literary identity, is that he was accustomed to speaking English at home, while conversing in Afrikaans with other relatives.

The pertinent features of his academic and work career can be briefly traced: he left school in 1956, and then studied English and mathematics at the University of Cape Town (BA 1960), after which he moved to England to work in computers in 1962. He stayed until 1965, working as a programmer, during which period he wrote a Master's thesis on Ford Madox Ford (MA awarded by the University of Cape Town in 1963). In 1963 he married

1

Philippa Jubber (1939–91), with whom he had two children, Nicolas (1966–89) and Gisela (b. 1968). (The early death of his son was clearly an influence on his novel *The Master of Petersburg* (1994).)

In 1965 Coetzee returned to academia: he moved to the USA, to the University of Texas at Austin, on a Fulbright exchange programme, where he produced his doctoral dissertation on the style of Samuel Beckett's English fiction, completed in 1969. He taught at the State University of New York at Buffalo from 1968 to 1971, during which period he worked on his first novel *Dusklands*. Coetzee's application for permanent residence in the USA was denied, and he returned to South Africa to take up a teaching position at the University of Cape Town in 1972. Following successive promotions, he became Professor of General Literature at his alma mater in 1983, and then Distinguished Professor of Literature from 1999 to 2001.

Coetzee has held various visiting professorships in the USA – at Johns Hopkins University, Harvard University, and the University of Chicago, among others. He has won many prestigious literary awards, including the Booker Prize (twice: in 1983 and 1999), the *Prix Etranger Femina* (1985) and the Jerusalem Prize (1987). His international prominence with a wider readership beyond academia was secured with the publication of *Disgrace* in 1999, and consolidated with the award of the Nobel Prize in 2003. Yet the international acclaim that greeted *Disgrace* was not matched by its reception in South Africa. The treatment of the gang rape of a white woman by black men, as a figure for an aspect of postcolonial historical process, caused a furore, and this seems to have had a bearing on Coetzee's decision to turn his back on South Africa: in 2002 he emigrated to Australia to take up an honorary research fellowship at the University of Adelaide.

There is a biting irony in this. Whereas the censorship board in the apartheid era had scarcely been troubled by Coetzee's subtle interrogations of the colonial psyche, the ruling ANC in the new South Africa was incensed by *Disgrace*, and moved to condemn its depiction of black violence, finding therein a racist perspective and the promotion of racial hatred. It is not clear whether or not Coetzee had already decided to leave South Africa; but this reception must surely have concentrated his mind.

To amplify some of these sparse details we must turn to the autobiographical elements in the writer's work, and the paradox that a very private writer has begun to expose intimate details of his life – or at least to invite speculation on these details. Formerly known as a writer who did not consider himself a public figure, someone in the public domain, he has now made 'the life', or the question of articulating the life, an aesthetic focus of his work. In relation to the first half of Coetzee's career, it seemed that the privacy of the man, his elusiveness, was also indicative of the nature of his literary project, with its emphasis on textuality, on novels as discursive events in the world, beyond the author's controlling hand. That judgement is in need of revision now that the writing project is linked to a kind of performance of the self.

Here we must turn to those two hybrid works that inhabit the border between fiction and autobiography, *Boyhood* and *Youth*. The 'Coetzee figure' that emerges from these books is often unpleasant, even disreputable (this is especially so in *Youth*). The oddity of this confessional gesture raises – and seems intended to raise – a host of questions about the relationship between fiction, autobiography, philosophy and confession. Such questions can, in themselves, prove revealing about Coetzee's identity; but these books also contain some explanation and contextualization of the author's familiar concerns. One such is Coetzee's preoccupation with his own ethnicity.

The question of identity, as a literary as well as an ethnic matter, has proved problematic for many white South African writers, especially those who, like Coetzee, have been based in South Africa. Coetzee is not an Afrikaner, but a white South African inhabiting a very particular margin, since his background partly distances him from both Afrikaner as well as English affiliations. Yet Coetzee's own comments on his ethnic identity show him to be intensely aware of the slipperiness of his position, and of the historical guilt that connects colonial and postcolonial experience. Although he felt no affinity with contemporary Afrikaner identity in the apartheid years, Coetzee admitted that he could be branded 'Afrikaner', on the basis of historical connection, and as a way of identifying his guilt by association with the crimes committed by the whites of South Africa. Coetzee has indicated that his writing sometimes draws its validity from this sense of complicity.

In *Boyhood: Scenes from Provincial Life* (1997) this particular issue of ethnicity, which is one of the key themes of the book, is put into context for us. Coetzee offers a series of autobiographical sketches, writing in the third person, and using the present tense, his trademark fictional mode. There is a narrow historical focus – the book traces episodes in the life of this boy from the age of ten to the age of thirteen (with some earlier recollections) – yet, if the sketches are taken at face value (and I will be suggesting a major caveat to this in due course), then a great deal about Coetzee's early years can be gleaned.

What distinguishes Coetzee's use of the present continuous tense in this book, from the uses to which it is put in his fiction, is the subject matter: a childhood memoir. This is not an obvious point about the difference between fiction and non-fiction, but an observation about the *fit* between the treatment of childhood experience and the effects generated by the present continuous. The sense of duration (and, often, boredom) associated with childhood is aptly caught by this mode of writing. It is also a way of dignifying the truism that the child is always present in the adult: the present tense of *Boyhood* conveys that sense of the continuing importance of the formative experiences described.

The experience of growing up in the South African town of Worcester is presented as one of endurance. The young Coetzee preferred Cape Town (where the family previously lived), and hankers after life on the farm in the Karoo – the arid, semi-desert plateau in Cape Province – owned by an Afrikaner uncle, and which he associates with happy holiday memories. The austere housing estate in Worcester that is his home makes a sorry comparison.

Coetzee's father emerges from this book in a bad light; but, on reflection, is a more sympathetic figure. (This, coupled with the intense relationship between Coetzee and his mother, creates a faint Lawrentian echo.) We understand that the father loses his government job in Cape Town as 'Controller of Letting' when the Nationalists come to power, for political reasons (he is not a Nationalist supporter), and that the removal to Worcester to work as a bookkeeper for Standard Canners (he is actually a lawyer, though has not practised since 1937) is a consequence of victimization. By the end of the book, however, the father has sunk into alcoholism, and has brought debt and disgrace upon the family, after their return to Cape Town and his failed attempt to restart his legal career.

As we have seen, a crucial aspect of Coetzee's identity, amplified in this book, is his bilingual status as both Afrikaans and English-speaking, but belonging to a family that clearly dissociates itself from the Afrikaner group. This is a form of self-exile that places them on the margins of South African life, since 'African' and 'Afrikaner' became the important poles between which the political tussle in the latter half of the twentieth century took place. Yet there is also social ambition in the parents' affiliation, and in their choice to educate Coetzee in English.

At his new school in Worcester, the young Coetzee is confronted with a question about his religion, and, coming from a family that does not practise religion, he is unable to respond appropriately. Asked, impatiently, by a teacher (and, we assume, a member of the Dutch Reformed Church) if he is 'a Christian or a Roman Catholic or a Jew', he plumps for Roman Catholic (*B*, p. 19). This gives him extra free time in the playground, while the Christians go off to assembly, but means he is bullied (together with the Jewish boys) when the Afrikaners return. It is this kind of experience that produces a deep antipathy to the Afrikaner identity, and a fear of being made to conform to it: 'the thought of being turned into an Afrikaans boy, with shaven head and no shoes, makes him quail. It is like being sent to prison, to a life without privacy' (*B*, p. 126). Even so, he discovers a facility in speaking Afrikaans in his extended family setting (associated with the freedom of his uncle's farm) that makes him feel as if 'all the complications of life seem suddenly to fall away'. Yet the childish appeal of seeming to become 'at once another person' (*B*, p. 125) is really of a piece with his desire for independence, and his refusal of the full implications of Afrikaner identity, which would deprive him of that crucial sense of 'privacy': 'he cannot live without privacy' (*B*, p. 126). There is a particular political dimension to this, and to his parents' resistance of the Afrikaans language. In response to the 'rumours that the government is going to order all schoolchildren with Afrikaans surnames to be transferred to Afrikaans classes', talked about by his parents 'in low voices', he formulates a plan: if ordered out of his English class by an inspector he will cycle home and refuse to return to school; and will 'kill himself' if his mother betrays him (*B*, pp. 69–70).

There are several elements in the portrayal of the young Coetzee that contribute to his sense of independence, or, the refusal to conform; and this prefigures the sense of resistance that becomes the key characteristic of the writer. One notable instance of this refusal to conform (and one instance of the book's humour) is the boy's whimsical predilection for things Russian. At the outset of the Cold War, and in a country in which communism is soon to be criminalized, this is evidently a startling and precocious preference for a young boy. His parents' disapproval does not cause him to relinquish his fascination with Russia; merely to turn it 'into a secret' (*B*, pp. 27–8).

An intriguing part of the memoir, already alluded to above, is the young Coetzee's deep attraction to the family farm in the Karoo, which passed to his uncle on the death of his grandfather: 'the farm is called Voëlfontein, Bird-fountain; he loves every stone of it, every bush, every blade of grass . . . it is not conceivable that another person could love the farm as he does' (*B*, p. 80). This formative experience was clearly an inspiration for *Life and Times of Michael K*, where the love of/identification with the farm is honed into an ethical vision. As we have seen, the freedom of Voëlfontein is associated with his facility in speaking Afrikaans; but there is no sense in which the appeal of the farm also embodies a cultural 'pull' he otherwise resists, or that the love of it is associated with an atavistic desire for possession of the land. Indeed, the particular linguistic inflection the young Coetzee associates with the farm suggests something much more positive, a 'slapdash mixture of English and Afrikaans' that is the extended family's 'common tongue when they get together' at Christmas:

> It is lighter, airier than the Afrikaans they study at School, which is weighed down with idioms that are supposed to come from the *volksmond*, the people's mouth, but seem to come only from the Great Trek, lumpish nonsensical idioms about wagons and cattle and cattle-harness. (*B*, p. 81)

The family tongue is a hybrid, situated against the odious ideology otherwise associated with Afrikaner culture in *Boyhood*.

This is, of course, also the child's rose-tinted view, which is partly justified by the treatment of the 'coloured people' who work the farm, a treatment that is more equitable than the young Coetzee has observed in racial relations in Worcester. A stronger burgeoning sense of racial justice is implicit in the boy's reactions throughout. Indeed, Coetzee assigns to his younger self an understanding of historical injustice in his perception of Cape 'Coloureds', 'fathered by whites ... upon the Hottentots'. He also knows that 'in Boland the people called Coloured are not the great-great-grand-children of Jan van Riebeeck or any other Dutchman ... They are Hotten-tots, pure and uncorrupted. Not only do they come with the land, the land comes with them, is theirs, has always been' (*B*, p. 62). In one telling episode, he is given some money to take his friends for an ice cream in a café, as a birthday treat; but the occasion is spoiled by 'the ragged Coloured children standing at the window looking in at them.' Their faces betray no 'hatred'; rather, they are 'like children at a circus, drinking in the sight, utterly absorbed, missing nothing'. Even if these children are chased away, 'it is too late, his heart is already hurt' (*B*, pp. 72–3). This is an arresting turn of phrase that successfully conveys the ambivalence of the moment, the boy's disappointment shot through with an incipient sense of guilt. It is a brilliant snapshot, the privilege being the element that simultaneously facilitates the pleasure, and sustains the inequality that undermines that pleasure. The older Coetzee is implying an awareness of this contradiction in his memory of his 'hurt' heart. And, of course, in the implied analogy with circus animals Coetzee assesses the privileged situation of himself and his friends as a kind of aberration, a form of fascinating exoticism.

The portrayal of the relationship with the mother is at the heart of this memoir: she is presented as the embodiment of maternal self-sacrifice, something the young Coetzee simultaneously desires in her, yet resents. The focus here is the contradictory and often unpleasant responses of the boy, detailed in the kind of excoriating confessional style that characterizes both of Coetzee's memoirs. We have a sense of a boy whose self-importance and coldness are both caused by having been spoiled at his mother's hands.

In the light of Coetzee's later connections between ethics and Christianity – a form of secular appropriation – the younger Coetzee's reaction to a biblical reading from the Gospel of Luke is intriguing. The reading (Luke 24: 5–6) describes the moment when the sepulchre is found to be empty, Jesus having risen. The boy does not like to hear these verses read, because 'if he were to unblock his ears and let the words come through to him, he knows, he would have to stand on his seat and shout in triumph. He would have to make a fool of himself forever' (*B*, p. 142). In an avowed unbeliever (*B*, p. 143), it is a reaction that demands attention. It implies the sensitivity of the boy to a particular kind of sentiment; but it is also a moment that reveals the unreliability of the memoir, the childhood perspective infused with the adult sensibility.

This ambivalence inevitably colours our perception of the book as a portrait of the artist as a boy. The later memoir *Youth* gently punctures the artistic pretensions of Coetzee as a 'youth'; and in *Boyhood* there is one arresting passage that identifies his creative aspirations. Bored by the topics presented for him in composition classes – sport, road safety, highwaymen – he articulates a desire to discover a more powerful topic:

> What he would write if he could . . . would be something darker, something that, once it began to flow from his pen, would spread across the page out of control, like spilt ink. Like spilt ink, like shadows racing across the face of still water, like lightning crackling across the sky. (*B*, p. 140)

The tone of this is hard to gauge. Setting aside the boyish desire to shock, or be dramatic, there is an implication of artistic potential that obviously suggests the perspective of the older Coetzee, commenting ironically on his younger self. Yet we cannot avoid taking this partly at face value; and we may do so, especially because of the way this passage echoes the final paragraph of *Foe*, where something is unleashed from Friday's mouth that implies the unstoppable and awesome power of postcolonial history. What is particularly noteworthy here is that Coetzee suggests that an aspect of that sublime/ awesome discourse will be an aspect of his own writing.

Inevitably, there is a dual perspective in this kind of autobiographical recollection, the mature artist projecting backwards onto his younger self certain notions that may or may not have been present in a frame of mind that is unrecoverable. What makes this routine duality particularly problematic in Coetzee's memoir is that he cultivates it, holding it up as a stylistic feature for the reader's attention. An early example of this is a description of the boy walking beside his mother. He considers that he 'probably looks quite normal', but reports an inner apprehension that suggests otherwise: 'he thinks of himself scuttling around her like a beetle, scuttling in fussy circles with his nose to the ground and his legs and arms pumping. In fact he can think of nothing about himself that is still. His mind in particular darts about here and there all the time' (*B*, p. 59). For a writer influenced by Kafka, the re-imagining of himself as a beetle in a family situation is arch. The description also undermines itself: the lucid 'external' view suggests a form of self-knowledge that cannot plausibly come from a mind that 'darts about . . . all the time'.

The point here is that we can detect not simply an artist's re-articulation of childhood experience, but a deliberate reminder that it is, indeed, a re-articulation. The effect is to make the idea of truth or veracity in the memoir subject to doubt, so that the emphasis of the writing is sometimes to question the memoir as a mode of writing. In this respect, *Boyhood* takes its place in Coetzee's series of problematic treatments of confessional writing. (The two novels written prior to the memoir, *Age of Iron* (1990) and *The Master of Petersburg* (1994), are the key texts.)

However, if one effect of *Boyhood* is to invite questions about the possibility of truth in autobiographical writing, questions that chime with some of Coetzee's fictional preoccupations, the memoir does still work differently. It is a form of hybrid, in which the author's fictional style is refashioned to engage with personal memory, and this makes the effects of the book very uncertain, but not necessarily less 'believable' than in a more conventional memoir. If the possibility of retrieving childhood memories is made subject to doubt, that use of the present continuous in this context makes this less relevant. As we have seen, the use of the present continuous serves to emphasize, implicitly, the continuity between child and adult, so that the memories projected backwards have a value in themselves. The focus then becomes what the *adult* makes of his formative experiences, and the way they are now woven into his narrative of 'the artist as a young boy'. In this respect, the memoir can be taken as 'reliable'.

The most obvious instance of dual perspective occurs towards the end of the book, and this is the keynote moment of the work. Coetzee here projects onto his thirteen-year-old self the ability, momentarily, to 'see the world as it really is'. In particular, the pubescent Coetzee is credited with the ability to see himself through the eyes of a passer-by, appearing no longer as 'a child, too big for that now, too big to use that excuse, yet still as stupid and self-enclosed as a child'. We can take this as an economical way for Coetzee to establish the life-stage for his boyhood self, in the convention of a memoir written in a confessional mode. It is the following perception assigned to the young Coetzee that is particularly noteworthy, however:

> In a moment like this he can see his father and his mother too, from above, without anger: not as two grey and formless weights seating themselves on his shoulders, plotting his misery day and night, but as a man and woman living dull and trouble-filled lives of their own. The sky opens, he sees the world as it is, then the sky closes and he is himself again, living the only story he will admit, the story of himself.
>
> (*B*, pp. 160–1)

This is another instance of dual perspective that works in a complex way. The stagey moment of clarity is a kind of wish-fulfilment, *possible* in the boy, though it is inconsistent with the selfishness that has been more usually associated with his point of view. It is improbable, then; and the improbability serves to expose the unreliability of the memoir – and all memoirs – and the difficulty of genuine secular confession. Yet the projection back of a doubtful epiphany of empathy also serves to reveal the empathy and understanding of the adult. It is a reshaping that is indicative of the later artist's consciousness; and, paradoxically, it becomes more genuine in the later Coetzee in inverse proportion to the degree it is felt to be a fabrication in the response of the boy: the desire that it *should have been so* is felt all the more.

Coetzee's second memoir, *Youth* (2002), exhibits the same rich ambivalence as *Boyhood*, its embodiment of the same literary conundrum – how to disentangle fact from fiction – being central to its effects. Indeed, the literariness of the work is signalled in the publisher's categorization of the work as 'fiction', and by the blurb that, in contrast to the dust jacket of *Boyhood*, makes no reference to Coetzee's own life. Opportunistic marketing is one explanation for this playing down of the autobiographical element: this was Coetzee's first book since the phenomenally successful *Disgrace*, so there was a good publishing reason to tout *Youth* as a new novel. Technically, it is a companion piece to *Boyhood*, tracing a series of formative vignettes in the life of a South African student (plainly based on Coetzee's experiences) narrated from the central character's perspective, but in the third person using the present tense.

Youth covers the period from 1959, when Coetzee was a nineteen-year-old student in South Africa, through to 1964 when he was working in England, having left South Africa for London in 1962, in the wake of the Sharpeville massacre (1960). In his time in England Coetzee worked as a computer programmer (then a new profession), first for International Business Machines (IBM), and then for the British firm International Computers. He also researched and wrote his Master's thesis on Ford Madox Ford, which was actually awarded in 1963, though there is no indication of the success of the thesis in *Youth*. The parents have little prominence or significance in this work. This is chiefly for the obvious reason that the youthful Coetzee in this portrayal has left home; and his determination to cast off the burden of his South African identity necessarily involves a rejection of parental values. Even so, it is interesting to note how the implied sympathy for the father in *Boyhood* is entirely absent from *Youth*. The brief mention of the father brings only the fear of an adverse genetic inheritance, 'the strain of fecklessness' (*Y*, p. 122). Correspondence from his mother simply inspires astonishment that she has not understood his desire to avoid 'contact with South Africans' (*Y*, p. 125).

There are, however, particular literary echoes in the title that signal the brand of self-consciousness that governs the work, and which makes plausible the publisher's categorization of the book as 'fiction'. At first glance, it is Tolstoy's *Youth* that seems the obvious point of reference: like Coetzee's book, Tolstoy's is based on the author's experiences and forms part of a sequence (a trilogy in Tolstoy's case). Tolstoy, like Coetzee, presents his earlier self in an unfavourable light, which makes this an important antecedent.

It is the other intertext, however, that may reveal a still more intriguing connection, in this case as a form of counterpoint. Conrad's short story 'Youth' is evidently evoked by Coetzee's choice of title, and the Conrad piece offers an ironic contrast to the purport of Coetzee's project. In 'Youth', Marlow (whose voyages resemble Conrad's own) tells the tale of his 'first voyage to the East', which is also his 'first voyage as second mate' ('*Youth*', '*Heart of Darkness*' and '*The End of the Tether*', Collected Edition (London: Dent, 1967), p. 4). It is a tale of heroic elemental struggles, first with a leaky vessel in stormy seas, and then with a cargo fire and explosion that eventually sinks the ill-fated craft. Marlow's youthful verve, fascination with the idea of the exotic East, and infatuation with the romance of the sea, are all proof against the hardships and disappointments of the voyage. Marlow reflects on the appeal of this formative experience, where burgeoning personal responsibility and the encounter with an exotic other come together, a feeling encapsulated in the moment when he first encountered 'the East', in the form of a verdant bay, glittering sands and a crowded jetty: 'And this is all that is left of it! Only a moment; a moment of strength, of romance, of glamour – of youth!' (p. 42). The feeling, conditioned by the sense of evanescence, is further punctured by the frame-narrator of the story, who is one of the friends listening to Marlow's tale: 'our weary eyes looking still, looking always, looking anxiously for something out of life, that while it is expected is already gone – has passed unseen, in a sigh, in a flash – together with the youth, with the strength, with the romance of illusions' (p. 42).

Implicit in this puncturing of illusions is an acknowledgement of the ambivalence embedded in colonial experience, where an uncomplicated fascination with the exotic is associated with the naïve, the youthful perspective. Marlow's desperate rescue, in a form of lifeboat, following the sinking of the main vessel – and as an object of scorn and fascination himself – plainly undermines the persisting excitement he associates with the experience, even though he fails to reach the anticipated exotic destination of Bangkok. To the extent that Marlow's experiences are based on Conrad's, there is a layer of authorial self-puncturing in this. These are the elements that Coetzee exaggerates in *Youth*, with great ironic effect; and the literary echo insists on a form of postcolonial reworking of Conrad's story. It is a reworking because, in Conrad's 'Youth', the sense of some kind of transcendent experience in the young Marlow's first encounter with the Orient still hangs in the air: indeed, the ambivalent ending depends upon its persistence. In Coetzee's *Youth*, there is no element of transcendence associated with youth; but there is a form of ambivalence, harder-edged, emerging from the exposure of the autobiographical illusion.

If we do read *Youth* as an autobiography, however, some important aspects of Coetzee's life seem to come into focus. The book covers a narrow period of his life, between the ages of nineteen and twenty-four. It may not seem inappropriate for a young man in this phase of life to be preoccupied with personal and sexual relationships; but the 'John' of this narrative emerges with no credit at all from his encounters with women. In the most shocking of these episodes, he meets his cousin Ilse and her friend Marianne, students from South Africa on holiday in Europe, and emerges as a sexual predator. He sleeps with Marianne, who is a virgin, and proves himself hopelessly ineffectual when the bleeding caused by their intercourse does not stop. He is concerned as much with his own situation as with her health and, on reflection, he considers himself to have 'behaved like a cad', as he attempts 'to fit' the episode 'into the story of his life that he tells himself' (*Y*, p. 130).

We may, however, not always feel inclined to accept these accounts – the story that he tells himself – since there are sometimes mitigating circumstances. In his first extended relationship, for example, he is effectively appropriated by the nurse Jacqueline, who is older than him, and who has

psychological problems. His coldness towards her (the quality that is associated with him throughout the book) is partly explained by our sense that
he is simply out of his depth. There is, however, a pattern to these failed
relationships, which founder usually because John is too immature to accept
his responsibility. When a girlfriend in Cape Town, Sarah, becomes preg-
nant, for example, he leaves it to her to arrange (and pay for) an illegal
abortion, realizing that he 'emerge[s] ignominiously' from the episode: 'how
can he who is still a child bring up a child?' Even here, however, we have a
glimpse of the literary game that Coetzee is engaged in, when John 'prays
[Sarah] will never tell the story to anyone' (*Y*, p. 35). If it is a true story, he
has now betrayed his own hope.

An important aspect of the book is the delineation of John's political
consciousness. Immediately following the sense of shame over his failure to
take responsibility for Sarah's pregnancy, we are given an account of events
following the Sharpeville massacre, so that John's reaction is already tainted
by our developing sense of his incomplete and immature self. In the period
of unrest following Sharpeville there are strikes and marches, one of which
interrupts a mathematics tutorial John is conducting, when the campus is
closed to allow a large demonstration organized by the Pan-African Congress
(PAC) to pass (and to prevent any students from joining the marchers
(*Y*, p. 38). John's reaction is conditioned by the identification of the march as
PAC-sponsored: 'The PAC is not like the ANC. It is more ominous. *Africa
for the Africans!* Says the PAC. *Drive the whites into the sea!*' John's immediate panic and sense of self-preservation is the dominant mood: '*Will the
ships still be sailing tomorrow? –* that is his one thought. *I must get out before
it is too late!*' (*Y*, pp. 38–9).

There follows some further panic at the thought of receiving a call-up
notice and being sent to a training camp alongside 'thuggish Afrikaners,
eating bully-beef out of cans, listening to Johnnie Ray on Springbok
Radio' (*Y*, pp. 39–40). Coetzee manages to condense a good deal of self-
condemnation into this section, the ease with which he conjures a stereotype
of the philistine Afrikaner being particularly arresting. At the beginning of
the next chapter John is in Belsize Park, an ellipsis that damns him pretty
thoroughly. Where the Sharpeville massacre was a wake-up call to many
liberal opponents of apartheid, now forced to accept that non-violent
resistance was futile, for John the episode is simply the spur to flee.

John's political cynicism takes on a more considered dimension. Notable,
here, is his reaction to a copy of *The African Communist*, a magazine banned
in South Africa, and which he chances upon in a branch of the bookshop
Dillons. The generation of radical anti-apartheid intellectuals associated with

The African Communist are (in effect) summarily dismissed by John, who recognizes, amongst the contributors, the names of his Cape Town peers, lazy, privileged and hedonistic students who he is surprised to see 'writing authoritative-sounding articles about the economics of migratory labour or uprisings in rural Transkei'. The reaction is complex in that it admits of a degree of (natural) peer-group jealousy, especially convincing in a would-be writer. There is also the tacit admission that these contributors might, indeed, be authoritative in these matters: 'where, amid all the dancing and drinking and debauchery, did they find the time to learn about such things?' (*Y*, p. 57). Yet, perhaps in the mature Coetzee, there is also a more significant element of cynicism concerning the privileged class of the intelligentsia, presuming to speak for/on behalf of the oppressed.

At the time of the Cuban missile crisis, John attends a major CND rally in Trafalgar Square (following a march from the nuclear weapons station at Aldermaston), 'taking care to stay on the fringes as a way of signalling that he is only an onlooker' (*Y*, pp. 84–5). In this episode, as elsewhere in the book, historical events are condensed, and focused on John's personal concerns. His response to the speakers' fears of nuclear annihilation, with Britain as a target, is, once more, a form of apolitical withdrawal: 'where can one turn to be free of the fury of politics? . . . Should he throw up everything and catch the next boat to Stockholm? . . . Does Sweden need computer programmers?' (*Y*, p. 85). The irony is that his programming work with International Computers has a military application. He is required to spend time at Aldermaston, installing the routines for which he is responsible, and becoming complicitous 'in the Cold War, and on the wrong side too' (*Y*, p. 163).

It is, however, the stigma of being a white South African that determines John's apolitical views. He reports voicing the opinion that 'the Russians ought to invade South Africa . . . take Verwoerd and his cronies captive, line them up against a wall, and shoot them'. What comes next does not concern him, 'the rest is politics, and he is not interested in politics'. This curious mix of outrage and wilful political naivety is a consequence of personal frustration: 'South Africa is like an albatross around his neck. He wants it removed, he does not care how, so that he can begin to breathe' (*Y*, pp. 100–1).

The creative dimension to this sense of being stifled by politics and the badge of ethnicity is key; and that sense of imprisonment is felt, revealingly, when the would-be poet first turns his hand to prose. His first story is set in South Africa, which 'disquiets him', as it undermines his determination to flee the country: 'South Africa was a bad start, a handicap. An undistinguished rural family, bad schooling, the Afrikaans language: from each of these component handicaps he has, more or less, escaped' (*Y*, p. 62). The reader familiar with Coetzee's oeuvre will recognize that the consequences of these 'component handicaps' inform his novels in important ways, and that the immature tension between the felt political straitjacket and the desire for unfettered creativity is the tension that informs the work of the mature artist.

As a student in South Africa, John prepares himself intellectually through a targeted programme of reading to ensure 'he will not arrive in Europe a provincial bumpkin'. Following the authority of Eliot and Pound, he concludes that 'civilization since the eighteenth century has been an Anglo-French affair' (*Y*, p. 25). While this sets up a sustained ironic portrait of the artist as a young man, it also sounds the note of Eurocentric literariness that underpins much of Coetzee's work, albeit in a rich and complex manner.

John's uncertainty concerning 'what the study of literature ought to be' is interesting in the light of Coetzee's continued suspicion of how critical language can seek to master literary texts. His preference, as a student, for 'the philological side of English' suggests that the inclination towards systemic modes of study – as evidenced in John/Coetzee's aptitude for mathematics and computer programming – is a deep personal preference (*Y*, pp. 26–7). When John uses a computer programme to generate poetry, and has a South African friend publish these 'pseudo-poems' in a magazine, he enjoys brief notoriety in Cape Town 'as the barbarian who wants to replace Shakespeare with a machine' (*Y*, p. 161).

Coetzee's inclination towards systemic modes of analysis issues in his austere work on pattern and repetitiveness in Samuel Beckett (see *Doubling the Point*, pp. 17–53); and it is interesting to read of John's first encounter with Beckett's fiction, which makes Ford seem like a 'stuffed shirt' in comparison. *Watt* is the book that facilitates the discovery, a work in which he finds 'no clash, no conflict, just the flow of a voice telling a story, a flow continually checked by doubts and scruples, its pace fitted exactly to the pace of his own mind. *Watt* is also funny, so funny that he rolls about laughing' (*Y*, p. 155). This is revealing about Coetzee's own inspiration and development, of course; but it also supplies a clue about how to read *Youth*. Self-evidently, *Youth* is characterized as the flow of a voice fitted to the author's mind, and constantly checked by doubts; what is not immediately obvious is that it is often funny, most especially when those doubts and scruples give way to open self-mockery.

The self-puncturing makes for a complex tone, and – as in *Boyhood* – this is crucial to the effects of this memoir/novel. There are clues along the way that John is being presented in the most critical light possible. For example, his self-centred response to the post-Sharpeville PAC march inspires in him an instant desire to flee South Africa, checked only by the thought that he would be severely disadvantaged were he to flee 'without taking his degree' (*Y*, p. 40). Chapter four ends with this double dose of self-preservation, the latter apparently paralyzing the former, thus confining him within South Africa until he graduates. Yet the next chapter opens with the young Coetzee in a London bedsit, a temporal compression that implies he has indeed escaped South Africa impulsively, immediate personal fear having overcome prudent self-interest. John thus emerges as being motivated by fear. When, on the following page, we discover that he does indeed have a degree ('in mathematics and English' (*Y*, p. 42)), we realize that he must have acted more cautiously; yet the impression of cowardice, implied by the narrative ellipsis, is not entirely effaced. In this way – and this is representative of the book as a whole – Coetzee contrives to depict his youthful self in as poor a light as possible. Partly, this has to do with his ongoing preoccupation with the confessional mode, and the attempt to get beyond the self-interest that can always be said to taint a confession; but there is also an important writing strategy at work here, which unsettles the plausibility of the self-portrait.

This process of letting the reader in on the business of self-parody is most evident in the presentation of John's artistic pretensions. A running theme in the book is the simple equation John draws between debauchery/sexual transportation and art, in pursuit of the stereotypical life of bohemian Europe. His studied coldness then becomes a potential defence against the 'women who flock after artists', yearning 'to be licked by tongues of flame' while simultaneously desiring 'to quench the fever and bring down the artist to common ground'. Self-justification begets a form of mild misogyny (*Y*, p. 31). The self-justification mutates: when John finds himself working in computers, and living in sobriety, he compares himself unfavourably with those poets who, in the previous century, 'deranged themselves with opium or alcohol' to unleash 'their visionary experiences'. He is comforted by the examples of T. S. Eliot, Wallace Stevens and Franz Kafka, all of whom had desk jobs: 'there is no dishonour in electing to follow Eliot and Stevens and Kafka' (*Y*, pp. 59–60).

The funniest instance of this appropriation of literary influence is John's account of how he, like his contemporaries, is influenced by D. H. Lawrence: 'from Lawrence they were learning to smash the brittle shell of civilized convention and let the secret core of their being emerge.' Coetzee then has some fun with the idea of the 'dark core' to which girls now expect to be taken, and John's nervousness about such girls: 'with some of them he would have liked to go to bed, that he could not deny – only by bringing a woman to her own dark core, after all, could a man reach his own dark core – but he was too scared'. He would be 'too puny', he reckons, to survive the 'volcanic' ecstasies that would result (*Y*, pp. 67–8). The idea of Lawrentian sexual transportation is then adapted by John into a fantasy of the artistic Muse, characterized as the Destined One, with whom he might experience a transformative 'ecstasy bordering on death'. He resolves to keep himself ready for the encounter (*Y*, p. 93).

A connection is clearly made between John's deluded perception of himself as a poet and his immature sexuality, so that when he makes 'a connection between the end of yearning and the end of poetry', and 'his failure as a writer and his failure as a lover', the reader sees the culmination of a rites-of-passage narrative in which the central character must relinquish a delusion about sexual identity and a related idea about writing (*Y*, p. 166). It is a simple message about self-discovery and independence, and the pointlessness of trying to emulate the careers of other artists. When we read of John seeking to copy Ford's Provençal diet of fish, olive oil and garlic, by frying fish fingers in olive oil and seasoning them with garlic salt, the bathetic contrast between his own existence and his aspirational idea of the artistic life is at its plainest (*Y*, p. 136).

The young man's (not unnatural) preoccupation with sexuality, when not falsely sublimated, is exposed as something rather more basic. His view of dancing as 'merely a cover', a 'foreshadowing of intercourse', leads him to wonder 'why people bother with dancing at all' (*Y*, pp. 89–90). For the reader familiar with Coetzee's work, it is the correspondence here with an observation made by Jacobus Coetzee in *Dusklands* that strikes the loudest chord: it recalls Jacobus's account of being annoyed by the complexity of a Namaqua dance involving courtship behaviour, and his feeling that he would have been relieved to see 'the dancers . . . drop their pantomime and cavort in an honest sexual frenzy culminating in mass coitus' (*D*, p. 86). The deliberate echo of this perspective – that of Coetzee's brutal colonizer – thoroughly undermines John's pretensions; but it also underscores the self-conscious and literary dimension of *Youth*. Just as John's perspective has been predetermined by a host of literary encounters, and the way in which they are overwritten by experience, so is the depiction of John, as a form of excoriating self-analysis conducted by Coetzee, complicated by Coetzee's previous books. The recurring theme of historical complicity, embodied most emphatically in the figure of Jacobus Coetzee, is particularly pertinent here, since it suggests that John is being subjected to an extreme form of condemnation. And this is another way in which Coetzee builds in the idea of a resisting reader.

With some care it is certainly possible to extract from *Youth* some insights into Coetzee's artistic development. Another example of this is the discovery of the accounts of early European travellers to the Cape, in the Reading Room of the British Museum, which is plainly the point at which his first novel begins to gestate, even though this memoir does not look forward to the writing of that work. This travel writing inspires in John the desire to write a form of literary hybrid, a fictional travel book steeped in knowledge of the past, and so exuding 'the aura of truth' (*Y*, pp. 137–8). The reader with knowledge of Coetzee's career, then, can see the origins of his creative trajectory – and will clearly distrust the dismal self-portrait of a failed artist that *Youth* paints.

This is not, however, simply a question of forward projection. *Youth* itself has an important place in Coetzee's ongoing and various explorations of fictional modes, an element of the book that is signalled early on in this reflection: 'the question of what should be permitted to go into his diary and what kept forever shrouded goes to the heart of all his writing' (*Y*, p. 9). The voice of the older John – the persona we take to 'stand for' Coetzee – is heard here, tacitly announcing that the question of self-censorship has been a running theme in his writing career. The presence of a more mature voice overlaid on the youthful protagonist, whose thoughts are made to emerge from the narrative throughout, announces the vexed problem of voice that is familiar in all autobiography. But Coetzee exaggerates this problem of hindsight in a way that is also signalled here: for John, the question of inclusion and exclusion hinges on the problem of whether or not to censor 'ignoble emotions', the problem of knowing 'true feelings' given the transience of experience, and so on (*Y*, p. 10). It is soon obvious, however, that this memoir is based on a concentration of all that is ignoble in John, as a central feature of its explosion of the idea of the great artist. At one level, *Youth* is a formal experiment that exposes that false ideology, while simultaneously deconstructing the genre of the personal memoir. It is unsurprising that there has been no third instalment.

In a brief memoir called 'Remembering Texas' (*DP*, pp. 50–53), Coetzee recalls the phase of his life immediately following the period accounted for in *Youth*. As we have seen, he arrived in America in September 1965 (aged twenty-five) to undertake postgraduate studies (the PhD on Beckett) at the University of Austin, and to teach freshman English, with an annual stipend of $2,100. In the remarkable interview that concludes *Doubling the Point*, in which Coetzee speaks of himself in the third person (foreshadowing his books of 'memoir'), he consigns this period of his life to a particular phase of development. The 'formalistic analysis of Beckett' reveals a sympathetic correspondence between the young Coetzee and the 'period in Beckett's life when Beckett too was obsessed with form, with language as a self-enclosed game'. In recollection, Coetzee presents this as the instigation of a self-prescribed 'formalistic, linguistically based regimen' that was to last fifteen years. And the decision to 'quit computers in favor of an academic life' was, he avers, 'a life-saving decision' (*DP*, pp. 393–4).

In 'Remembering Texas' there is an emphasis on the professionalism in English Studies that confronts Coetzee, set against the dilettante lifestyle of the 'colonial teachers' he had encountered in South Africa, an education which had left him unable to distinguish literary criticism from 'book reviewing or polite talk about books' (*DP*, pp. 53, 50). In the retrospective interview, the discovery of this professionalism is presented as a form of salvation, and a staging post of self-definition that will lead to 'a more broadly philosophical engagement with a situation in the world' that the later Coetzee identifies with the writing of his important essay (1982–3) on confession ('Confession and Double Thoughts: Tolstoy, Rousseau, Dostoevsky', *DP*, pp. 251–93). This essay, he claims, is pivotal in his understanding of his personal development, marking the point where '*autre*biography shades back into autobiography' (*DP*, p. 394). It is intriguing that Coetzee's exercises in autobiography end, chronologically, where the important 'life-saving' phase begins; and that suggests they are very much works of 'autrebiography' following Coetzee's distinction, the felt distance between author and subject – demonstrable in the formal operations of those works – confirmed in the author's testimony.

In the most recent phase of his career, it is possible to see the interaction between personal guilt/responsibility and the 'engagement with a situation in the world' in a postcolonial perspective. The way in which 'late colonial' issues of personal complicity open out into the broader postcolonial context is especially noteworthy in the works published after Coetzee's move to Australia in 2002. In *Slow Man* (2005), for example, there seems to be a self-conscious attempt by Coetzee to relate his fictional preoccupations to his own position as an immigrant to Australia. The book's main concern is with authenticity, and in relation to national identity this is given a particular slant by the attempts of Paul Rayment (raised in France) to insert himself into the national history of his adopted country by amassing a collection of historical photographs, detailing the migrant experience in the nineteenth century. The question of belonging is thrown into uncertainty, however, by the role of the Jokić family, economic refugees from Croatia. This raises the sensitive question (for Australians) of how economic migrants should be received, in a nation built on the efforts of migrants; it also throws the issue of personal history and belonging into uncertainty. When Drago, the Jokić son, purloins one of Rayment's rare nineteenth-century images of migrant workers, and produces a digital forgery as a joke (with his own father's image superimposed), the possibility of a fluid national identity is raised.

If such fluidity would implicitly dismiss the pomposity of Rayment – who desires to carve out a role in the national life by bequeathing his photograph collection to the State Library in Adelaide (*SM*, pp. 48–9) – it would privilege the ongoing significance of the migrant in the social and cultural life of the nation, and also carve out a role for Coetzee. Read one way, this seems to be the tacit logic of a novel that might justify Coetzee's new affiliation. Yet the novel also reveals him to be acutely aware of the difficulties of belonging, and of wielding authority in cultural work, and this is given extensive treatment in the novel's metafictional strand, which sees the return of his creation Elizabeth Costello, here as the ostensible 'author' of the other characters in the novel. This familiar, and seemingly tired postmodernist gesture, is given a particular edge by Rayment's rejection of her as an 'outsider'. She is an outsider to the world of her own fiction, as much as Coetzee is an outsider to his new adopted country. In the final working-out of the novel, which sees Rayment dismissing Costello (*SM*, p. 263), there may be a tacit acknowledgement by Coetzee of his own displacement, and the new sense of inauthenticity that accompanies it.

It seems that part of the self-consciousness of the novel stems from Coetzee's own self-consciousness about his presumption to pronounce on Australian national identity. It is a very particular version of a familiar novelistic dilemma, and one which had haunted the work of the white novelist in the apartheid era: who is qualified to write about whom?

The author's concern with his own ethnicity – and his public role – is a point of focus in *Diary of a Bad Year* (2007), in which Coetzee appears to come very close to writing a directly autobiographical novel. The central character (JC) shares his initials and first name 'John'. Both Coetzee and JC are white South African writers, recent immigrants to Australia, and JC's books are also Coetzee's. (*Waiting for the Barbarians* is expressly mentioned.) However, there are also points of difference – JC is five or six years older than his creator, for example (*DBY*, p. 163) – and so JC starts to emerge as a development of the figure epitomized in Elizabeth Costello, the authorial persona that cannot be equated with Coetzee, even though we may be tempted, or even invited, to speculate on the extent to which these authorial figures are sometimes mouthpieces for Coetzee. A full engagement with the effects of *Diary of a Bad Year* makes us realize that this is part of the textual game, a device that opens up more important questions about the relationship between fiction and reality.

Even so, it is hard not to spot some heartfelt remarks, such as this reflection from JC, which we hear as Coetzee's later reflections on the sense of historical guilt felt by white South Africans of his generation: 'The generation of South Africans to which I belong, and the next generation, and perhaps the generation after that too, will go bowed under the shame of the crimes that were committed in their name' (*DBY*, p. 44).

Towards the end of *Diary of a Bad Year* there are two essays (part of the book is comprised of 'mini-essays') on artists of particular significance for Coetzee, J. S. Bach and Dostoevsky; and, again, it is hard not to read a personal element into the recorded feelings of JC. Discussing Dostoevsky, he makes reference to the chapter in *The Brothers Karamazov* 'in which Ivan hands back his ticket of admission to the universe God has created', which causes him to sob 'uncontrollably' (*DBY*, p. 223). JC goes on to investigate his reaction, which is not explicable in rational terms. Against Ivan's 'rather vengeful views', JC enunciates his own belief 'that the greatest of all contributions to political ethics was made by Jesus when he urged the injured and offended ... to turn the other cheek'. Puzzling his emotional vulnerability to Ivan's views, JC indicates that he has been affected by rhetorical effects rather than ethics or politics:

> Far more powerful than the substance of his argument, which is not strong, are the accents of anguish, the personal anguish of a soul unable to bear the horrors of this world. It is the voice of Ivan, as realized by Dostoevsky, not his reasoning, that sweeps me along.
>
> (*DBY*, p. 225)

This mini-essay rapidly undercuts the distinction between 'rhetoric' and ethics, emotion and reason, that it establishes at the outset. JC realizes that the Christian Dostoevsky, in realizing an anti-Christian sentiment in such moving terms, creates a 'battle pitched on the highest ground' (*DBY*, p. 226). It is such achievements, suggests JC, that enable the master Russian writers, Tolstoy and Dostoevsky both, to set the example of how an artist might become 'ethically better' (*DBY*, p. 227). This is a key literary episode for Coetzee. (It is briefly mentioned in *Youth*, though in more prosaic fashion when John stiffly records his disapproval of people 'who disobey the rules', because 'if the rules are ignored, life ceases to make sense: one might as well, like Ivan Karamazov, hand back one's ticket and retire' (*Y*, p. 97).)

The appropriation of Christian motifs or principles in the name of political ethics is a compelling idea for Coetzee, and a tendency that can be observed throughout his career. Perhaps the most eye-catching of these appropriations is the following published remark about violence and the crucifixion, from one of the interviews with David Attwell:

> Violence, as soon as I sense its presence within me, becomes intro-verted as violence against myself . . . I cannot but think: if all of us imagined violence as violence against ourselves, perhaps we would have peace. (Whether peace is what we most deeply want is another story.) Or, to explain myself in another way: I understand the Cruci-fixion as a refusal and an introversion of retributive violence, a refusal so deliberate, so conscious, and so powerful that it overwhelms any reinterpretation, Freudian, Marxian, or whatever, that we can give to it.

Coetzee goes on to say: 'I think you will find the contest of interpretations I have sketched here – the political versus the ethical – played out again and again in my novels'; and it is this gloss that situates the ethical impetus of his work very clearly in a complex post-Christian global moment (*DP*, p. 337). At the same time, it is a strikingly personal ethos, and one that chimes entirely with the impression we have of Coetzee: intellectually independent, ethically sensitive, yet acutely conscious of the complicities and ambivalences that surround him, as an academic and as a novelist.

Chapter 2

Coetzee's contexts

Coetzee's novels occupy a special place in South African literature, and this is a context that is inevitably brought to bear on much of his writing; yet his work has an influential bearing on the development of the novel more widely, into the twenty-first century, and this broader context of the 'internationalization' of the novel is increasingly relevant to the appreciation of his achievements. This chapter, then, considers both the historical context in which Coetzee's career unfolds, and the intellectual and ideological context that is part and parcel of his life and times.

For much of his career, Coetzee lived and worked in South Africa, under the apartheid regime until 1990, and then witnessing the political difficulties of the transition to democratic government. Until he emigrated to Australia in 2002, it was the South African context that permeated his writing. His work has embodied a form of intellectual challenge both to the late-colonial violence and oppression of apartheid, and to the dangers of retributive violence in the period of transition to democratic rule. In either case, his work has not always chimed with the popular mood: as an 'apartheid novelist', a term he would strongly resist, his work has been perceived as too oblique, with an insufficient political charge. Subsequently – and *Disgrace* is the most obvious example – he has been found to be out of kilter with the celebratory drive of new nation-building in post-apartheid South Africa. Yet, in both cases, his work displays a refusal to conform, or to allow the procedures of the novel to be conditioned by a normative drive.

As the previous chapter indicated, Coetzee's ethnicity – in the South African context – has had a crucial bearing on his literary identity. The question of a writer's identity is always a literary as well as an ethnic matter, a question of establishing the emergent or established, national or transnational, tradition into which his or her writing belongs. Neither is this simply a critical preoccupation: in the era of globalization, and the internationalization of the novel, it can be a literary theme in its own right. For the white South African writer, contributing to an emergent, yet wilfully manipulated and suppressed tradition, the relationship between the literary and ethnic aspects of identity is brought into sharp focus; and for Coetzee, it is the degree to which he is/is not associated with Afrikaner history and culture that is crucial.

Superficially, this might seem irrelevant: like any South African writer expressing condemnation of the apartheid regime, whether obliquely or directly, he is clearly distanced from that late-colonial Afrikaner identity with which the regime was associated. Yet, as we have seen, he is a white South African occupying a particular intellectual margin, since his background distances him from English, as well as Afrikaner affiliations. (He recalls the 'well-developed sense of social marginality' that he acquired in childhood, consequent upon his parents' indifference 'to the *volk* and its fate' (*DP*, p. 393).)

As his own recollections demonstrate, Coetzee has been acutely conscious of this issue, and of the slipperiness and ambivalence of the position he inhabits, on the cusp of colonial and postcolonial experience. He has suggested three applications of the term 'Afrikaner', in a discussion that has a direct bearing on his literary identity. The first of these is linguistic and cultural; and, by this measure, Coetzee feels himself distanced from Afrikaner speakers, since English is his first language. (Neither was he brought up in a family embedded in the Reformed Church, or other instruments of Afrikaner culture.) In the second application, 'Afrikaner' carries an ideological freight, whether it is the anti-British mood of the 1880s, or the anti-black Nationalism that became intensified during the last years of apartheid that is evoked. Anyone who does not share the political vision can withdraw (or be expelled from) the group.

The third application of the term, however, is more intractable. This is the external activity of naming someone on the basis of historical association. In this usage, Coetzee suggests, it is not in his gift 'to withdraw from the gang'. On the contrary, Coetzee has often cultivated a sense of complicity in his writing that draws on that aspect of his Afrikaner heritage that links him, historically, with colonial activity in Africa (*DP*, pp. 342–3). These reflections, taken from another of the interviews with David Attwell (from a group of interviews conducted between 1989 and 1991), establish an intellectual position that governed all of Coetzee's fiction into the early 1990s: the conviction that desire for political change cannot be allowed to overshadow, or displace, a more passive acceptance of historical guilt. This is not just a moral duty, but also a necessary acceptance of historical identity, upon which the genuine voice of a writer like Coetzee depends.

Coetzee was the first South African writer to produce overtly experimental and self-conscious fictions that draw their energies from the intellectual charge of the postmodernist/post-structuralist moment. For some, his reliance on European theoretical and literary models put him at the far end of the spectrum from those writers seeking to develop a 'pan-Africanist' model for South African writing. It is important to bear in mind, however, that European influences have long helped to shape the South African literary tradition, so he can be said to be working in this tradition. Even so, the influence on Coetzee of poststructuralist thinking places a stress on textuality not previously seen in his country's literature. Consequently, his works represent an implicit challenge to the orthodox privileging of realism in the South African novel. They also embody a challenge to the critical construction of postcolonial writing, since Coetzee occupies a very particular transitional site.

A crucial contextual force – or ideological pressure – felt by Coetzee is that which holds up a version of critical realism as the desirable norm for the novel in Africa. His resistance of 'history' should be seen as a challenge to this consensus rather than a reluctance to engage with the problem of historical representation.

In a talk from 1987, 'The Novel Today', Coetzee addresses the problem (in an apparently confrontational manner): 'in times of intense ideological pressure like the present', he argued, 'when the space in which the novel and history normally coexist like two cows on the same pasture, each minding its own business, is squeezed to almost nothing, the novel, it seems to me, has only two options: supplementarity or rivalry'. The crucial point here is that Coetzee locates his argument historically. He is describing a strategy – in this talk given in Cape Town during the 1986–90 State of Emergency – which is a direct response to late-apartheid South Africa. Specifically, he is challenging a sense that it is *de rigueur* for the committed anti-apartheid writer to tilt his or her writing towards a preconceived style of intervention: that is, the documentation of, the bearing witness to, the supplementation of, an agreed history. Rivalry with historical discourse, Coetzee suggests, will produce 'a novel that operates in terms of its own procedures and issues in its own conclusions, not one that operates in terms of the procedures of history and eventuates in conclusions that are checkable by history'. A concentration on the development of novelistic form – also a response to a precise political moment – embodies a rivalry with a pointed dialectical agenda, for such a novel would 'evolve its own paradigms and myths', in rivalry with (or 'even enmity' towards) history, which may consequently be demythologized.

Coetzee is arguing for a position that has affinities with a broader postcolonial revision of history. In his talk, he goes on to discuss the novel and history as different kinds of competing discourse, suggesting that his own role as a novelist is to counter the claims of history to primacy. Yet the extent to which this is also *atypical* of postcolonial revisionism must also be considered. Where the usual model is one in which a displaced or hidden history resurfaces in the process of decolonisation, Coetzee appears to be making a more fundamental challenge to the idea of history. For some commentators this challenge, which does not necessarily discriminate between Afrikaner mythology and anti-apartheid revisionism, might appear to lose its political edge. The perceived importance of a novelist such as Coetzee often turns on how this problem is viewed.

In finding his own way of articulating his context – in a historical and intellectual sense, simultaneously – Coetzee has recourse to the idea of a European literary genealogy as an example of a shared cultural language, that which might positively oppose the ideological force of 'history'. It is a resource that Coetzee must sometimes draw on as an ambivalent touchstone in his own fiction. It is ambivalent because Coetzee does not necessarily separate European culture from the field of colonial domination, so the recourse to a European tradition, in the battle with 'history', is already an interrogation of historical forces. (His key influences include Defoe, Beckett, Dostoevsky, Kafka, Hegel and Derrida.)

The decisive contextual issue is the problem of defining appropriately the site of creativity that Coetzee inhabits. My discussion here will amplify the account of Coetzee's interim position in a very precise corner of post-colonial writing: the literature of the 'post-colonizer', conceived as a transitional site between Europe and Africa. (Now qualified by the latest 'migrant' phase of his career.) It is in the light of this discussion, concerning the location of the writer, that his literary style must be evaluated. If his measured response to the trajectory of history 'out there' is deemed appropriate, the resultant turning inwards, and the preoccupation with specifically literary questions, also need to be justified historically. Indeed, Coetzee's intellectual concerns are invariably fitted to his context, implicitly if not explicitly.

Coetzee's intellectual influences, as an academic working in English Studies, have inevitably taken his work in the direction of those complex literary questions posed by the poststructuralist/postmodernist turn. This is the intellectual context that generates his oblique manner of expression, and which prompted criticism from those readers expecting a more direct engagement with social and political issues. It was the dominance of realism in South African fiction, as the necessary means of bearing witness to the operations of the state, especially during the apartheid era, that generated a norm against which Coetzee failed to measure up. Yet it was this norm, and the concept of realism that underpinned it, that Coetzee expressly defined himself against.

A key document in this connection is Nadine Gordimer's review of *Life and Times of Michael K* ('The Idea of Gardening'). Gordimer is widely perceived to belong to an opposing camp in the debate about realism in African fiction, having been influenced by Georg Lukács's prescriptions for 'critical realism' in the novel. In particular, her novels seek to enact the Lukácsian 'typification' of character, where the realization of individual characters is coupled with a recognition of a prevailing historical dynamic, so that public and private realms are rendered in a process of dialectical interaction. It is this concept of typicality that Gordimer uses as a yardstick in her evaluation of *Michael K*, arguing that K's passivity is historically unfaithful.

Coetzee is fundamentally opposed to this kind of prescriptive approach to the business of writing and evaluating novels. Rather than the evasion of history his writing is sometimes taken to be, his philosophy for writing can be seen as a very specific historical response. (As we have seen, in 'The Novel Today' Coetzee takes up this very issue, arguing that, in times of intense political pressure, the novelist has to choose between the two options of supplementarity or rivalry in engaging with history.)

In challenging the received wisdom that the committed anti-apartheid writer must find a mode that will facilitate the documentation of, or bearing witness to, an agreed history, Coetzee defends the novelist's art, promoting it as a form of independent resistance. We can see this as contributing to a broader postcolonial drive for the revision of history: if the novelist resists an agreed history, the revisionist view remains possible.

Coetzee's warning against the easy compromise, the writer's temptation to succumb to the pressure to conform and attempt a straightforward representation of history, carries an ethical imperative. Resisting the immediate history of social change also involves a steady evaluation of literary heritage. For Coetzee, the idea of a European literary genealogy may be the source of a shared cultural language, or the source of opposition to the force of brute history. Yet he is also sensitive to the ways in which European culture is linked to the business of colonial domination, so his recourse to a European tradition is already a means of interrogating longer-term historical forces. Taken together, Coetzee's responses to his political and intellectual contexts issue in a complex style of writing-against-itself.

Yet, an important aspect of Coetzee's imperative to find those literary and intellectual sources that will resist history is a sense of responsibility to literature. Implicit in this is a longer view of literature's function, which looks beyond the late-colonial situation in South Africa, even in the novels written during the brutal death throes of apartheid. At the same time, Coetzee manages to use his resources to reflect precisely on specific political moments, as he establishes the grounds on which his novels will reckon with history on their own terms.

Coetzee's literary self-consciousness issues in gestures that we might call 'textual decolonizations', however ambivalent they may be. (The implicit investigation of Defoe as the 'father' of the English novel, in *Foe*, is a rich example.) Intellectually, as an academic-novelist, Coetzee is a product of the post-structuralist/postmodernist turn; and, for a writer also situated in the complex field of postcolonial writing, he is sometimes perceived as being pulled in different directions, where the anti-colonial ethic is seen to be compromised by the new global imperialism of postmodernism.

On the face of it, there might appear to be good deal of common ground between postmodernism and postcolonialism, since both seem to be rooted in a rejection of the centre/margin hierarchical opposition. Consequently, both appear to share the project of dismantling Eurocentric master codes. Yet, for some commentators, these are superficial similarities that mask vital differences in both context and political orientation. Indeed, some examples of postmodernist expression are perceived to advance a form of cultural uniformity that denies the celebration of otherness that is the central achievement of postcolonial writing.

It is important, here, to preserve the distinction between postmodernity (a period) and postmodernism (the cultural response to it), so that, even if we perceive postmodernity to be a manifestation of late capitalism, the postmodernist writer or critic can still be seen to occupy a (partially) autonomous space in which to reflect. To be effective, the poststructuralist critic occupies the same space, in the broad understanding of 'postmodernism'. Yet, if postmodernism is often critical of postmodernity, it is also a product of it, so that autonomous space is squeezed. For some, postmodernism is symptomatic of its broader global moment, its critique rendered anodyne, if not invalid. For postcolonial theory, this is a potentially damaging charge, especially, for example, if the process of dismantling the codes that divide the self from the other is really a European export, based on the Western construction of the bourgeois subject. Even the conscious exploration of complicity, a common theme in the discourses of postmodernism and postcolonialism, can be viewed as a peculiarly Western crisis.

The poststructuralist appropriation of postcolonial texts might then be a form of cultural imperialism, based on the assumption of a shared decentring drive, which could be motivated quite differently. Indeed, we might expect the experience of colonization to produce a highly politicized 'decentring' impulse of a quite different hue to the more theoretical areas of the postmodern. While these objections carry considerable force in relation to some areas of postcolonial study, Coetzee's particular situation obliges us to view them in a less oppositional spirit. To begin with, the anxieties about the postmodern/postcolonial cusp supply a thematic core to his writing; moreover, the position of the white academic-writer in South Africa necessarily conflates postcolonialism and postmodernism, in a conjunction that defines a precise historical and intellectual context.

In a sense, Coetzee's position, with his determination to embrace complicity, allows us to sidestep the debate about the compromised position of postcolonialism as an intellectual field. It is then the *nature* of that complicity that becomes significant, rather than a dispute about the extent of it. Important in this connection is Simon During's distinction between the 'post-colonized', those who identify with the culture overlaid by imperialism, and by the language of the colonizer, and the 'post-colonizers', those who are embroiled in the culture and language of colonialism, even while they reject imperialism ('Postmodernism or Post-colonialism Today', p. 127). For the English-speaking writer in South Africa there is an extra complication, because the English language is not an imperialist tongue in any simple sense; and, in recent history, Afrikaans has been viewed as the imperialist language. (It was the enforced use of Afrikaans in teaching that led to the Soweto riots of 1976–7.) With this qualification, it seems appropriate to consider Coetzee as a 'post-colonizer' in During's sense, occupying that margin of postcolonial writing in which complicity is the necessary focus.

The idea of the post-colonizer facilitates the complex analysis of European influences within postcolonial writing, without the expectation that such influences will be straightforwardly ironized or parodied. Pertinent here is Helen Tiffin's definition of that branch of postcolonial culture where 'decolonization is process, not arrival' ('Post-Colonial Literatures and Counter-Discourse', p. 17). In such writing, European and local discourses are made to interact, in a dialectical relationship where European discourses are very much present, even while they are partly subverted or dismantled. This is entirely in tune with Coetzee's own formulation with regard to 'white writing' in South Africa as writing 'generated by the concerns of people no longer European, not yet African' (*WW*, p. 11).

The international significance of Coetzee may be explained with reference to his position as post-colonizer, since this is a literary identity that admits the presence and effects of colonialism in its world-view. His stature may derive from the power with which he speaks to a broad international readership – a readership with consciousness of a shared experience – while he simultaneously offers precise discursive interventions in one specific context. This combination of the general and the particular, in which South African experience is particularized, yet also made relevant to the international moment of decolonization, speaks to a moment of transition that may have achieved its full resonance in the 1990s.

The emphasis of this account of Coetzee's contexts brings together two main areas of pertinence: his intellectual context and his historical context. Another aspect of his writing that conjoins the two is allegory. Allegory, in fact, is a recurring theme in both postcolonial writing and criticism. Semiotics, one of the branches of literary theory with which Coetzee is familiar, places great emphasis on allegory, in its implication that all language – and all literature – is allegorical in that it constitutes a network of deferred meaning. In this account, the literary work comprises allusions to (and substitutions for) a referent that is unattainable.

Traditionally understood, allegory substitutes one plane of significance for another (thus, the animal fable of Orwell's *Animal Farm* thinly veils the actual political parallels); indeed, allegory is a mode originally used by the victims of religious or political persecution as a device for concealing transgressive, or heretical ideas. Yet this clearly is an insufficient explanation of Coetzee's use of allegory. Perhaps a traditional understanding of the device of allegory had a bearing on how Coetzee's work was assessed by the South African censors: as too indirect to represent a threat to the state (*DP*, p. 298). Coetzee is quite clear, however, that such a flat use of allegory has become anachronistic: 'the game of slipping Aesopian messages past the censor is ultimately a sterile one, diverting writers from their proper task' (*GO*, p. viii). In postmodernist expression, however, allegory becomes highly self-conscious, a mode which advances a radical investigation of its own grounding. (See Fredric Jameson, *Postmodernism, or, the Cultural Logic of Late Capitalism*.) In Coetzee's novels, this form of self-analysis, or 'undoing' of allegory, often serves to blur the distinction between the two parallel planes of significance – the allegorical and the literal referent. The way in which Coetzee's work constantly elides metonymic and metaphoric impulses can be understood as a signal that postmodern allegory is at work, since allegory inclines towards metaphor, while the mimetic code of writing is governed by metonymy.

Postcolonial allegory supplies the context for this more generalized and abstract theory of postmodern allegory, suggesting how the mode can perform pointed textual decolonizations. For Stephen Slemon, postcolonial allegory cultivates historical revisionism, since images of received history are alluded to through a process of allegorical correspondence, engaging the reader in a dialectic of discourses. Readers are invited to read received history alongside the fictional engagement of it, thus unsettling our perception of stability in the historical record ('Post-Colonial Allegory and the Transformation of History', pp. 158–63).

What makes this unstable form of allegory both more complex, and necessary, from a postcolonial point of view, is that a more static idea of allegory can be associated with the colonial project, as Slemon shows. Just as traditional allegory could be decoded when read alongside the correct master code, so did colonists, in a reverse impulse, project onto the objects of colonization their own master codes of interpretation. Thus, just as local flora and fauna would be 'discovered' with reference to a European taxonomy, so were native social codes and behaviour interpreted from the colonists' perspective. (Coetzee's essay 'Idleness in South Africa' is relevant here (*WW*, pp. 12–35).) It is this allegorizing tendency, as a root impulse in imperialism, that requires the radical interrogation of allegory as a viable mode in postcolonial writing. Throughout his oeuvre, Coetzee has repeatedly used an ambivalent form of allegory – as a mode written partly against itself – with the benign effect of exposing the closural tendency of colonial thinking. (In chapter 5, I consider Derek Attridge's important ideas on allegory in relation to Coetzee.)

The extent to which literary theory infiltrates Coetzee's novels can be gleaned from the example of *Life and Times of Michael K*, and the way in which that novel enacts ideas drawn from Derridean deconstruction. (Michael Marais's essay 'Languages of Power: A Story of Reading Coetzee's *Michael K*/ Michael K' is a good example of how critics have persuasively made such connections.) For example, the medical officer in part two of the novel makes an attempt at allegory (in an imagined address to Michael K) that suggests the entire novel is rooted in a deconstructive principle:

> Your stay in the camp was merely an allegory, if you know that word. It was an allegory – speaking at the highest level – of how scandalously, how outrageously a meaning can take up residence in a system without becoming a term in it. (*MK*, p. 166)

The allusion to the idea of infinitely deferred meaning also undermines the idea of allegory that is the basis of the illustration. Coetzee seems here to place the term 'allegory' under erasure, in accordance with that Derridean procedure in which terms are scored through: the procedure encapsulates a paradox in drawing attention to the inadequacy of terms that remain necessary for an idea to be thought through, much as the idea of allegory is simultaneously questioned and utilized in most of Coetzee's novels.

Another clear allusion is found in Michael K's cultivation of pumpkins and melons from seed, which evokes Derrida's version of textuality as 'dissemination', an unproductive process of repetitive semination that is certainly echoed in K's continually interrupted career as a cultivator, repeatedly denied a harvest. Derridean dissemination implies a principle of textual free play, freed from an originating author or pre-given meaning. Coetzee's implicit engagement with this idea, however, also implies a deconstruction of the idea of dissemination itself. K, for example, sidesteps the question of his role as father-originator, with respect to his seeds, by considering them as his brothers and sisters (*MK*, p. 113). K's thoughts about his genealogy embody a comparable disruption of the parental-originator, through the role of the mother figure, when he reflects, 'I come from a line of children without end':

> He tried to imagine a figure standing at the head of the line, a woman in a shapeless grey dress who came from no mother; but when he had to think of the silence in which she lived, the silence of time before the beginning, his mind baulked. (*MK*, p. 117)

There is plainly an allusion here to that hankering after origins that Derrida sees as a seminal flaw in Western metaphysics; yet such allusions have a 'surface' quality to them, and also a tendency to enact and question the paradoxes they throw up. In *Michael K* an authoritative principle is ultimately revealed, a principle of Being, rooted in the minimalist principle of survival embodied in K; and this unsettles the deconstructive principle of K's elusiveness in that he finally stands for something – the idea of Being, a state of existence prior to knowledge – that is at odds with the deconstructive principle. In a delightful paradox, Coetzee deconstructs the novel's reliance on figures and motifs drawn from deconstruction.

In *Foe* there is a comparable dual movement which betrays a concern about how the moment of poststructuralism, with its particular emphasis on questions of textuality, might itself be seen to embody a new form of intellectual imperialism, and a new form of colonization. This dual movement plays out as an internal debate about the dangers of extreme self-consciousness set against the persisting claims and pulls of realism. The novel's engagement of Defoe serves, partly, to challenge naïve perceptions of realism; and the novel, informed by poststructuralism, draws out some compelling implications about power and discourse for the postcolonial context. At the same time, however, the novel makes an appeal for the kind of transparent realism that is acknowledged to be no longer possible.

This typically Coetzean paradox brings to the fore the perception of substantiality and material being, implicitly raising the issue of how empathy might beget intervention – and the route through which this chain of associations is made requires a knowingly poststructuralist suspension of belief. The imprisoning nature of language games is made clear in the warning Foe gives Susan Barton: 'you must ask yourself, Susan: as it was a slaver's stratagem to rob Friday of his tongue, may it not be a slaver's stratagem to hold him in subjection while we cavil over words in a dispute we know to be endless?' (*F*, p. 150). In this we can hear the kind of warning that has become familiar in debates about poststructuralism and post-colonialism, that a circular and self-contained form of theorizing about discourse may be another kind of 'slaver's stratagem', even if it is advanced in the interests of decolonization.

The portrayal of Foe, however, finally returns us to the emphasis on textuality. When he argues that 'writing is not doomed to be the shadow of speech' he advances a poststructuralist tenet about the primacy of writing (*F*, p. 142). In such moments he seems closer to Coetzee than to Defoe, a gesture that produces an anachronistic composite writing persona that fits Coetzee's position and inheritance. When Foe explains that, 'in a life of writing books, I have often . . . been lost in the maze of doubting', he produces a precise metaphor for Coetzee's provisional postcolonial position (*F*, p. 135).

To the extent that poststructuralist thought is usually held to be the intellectual aspect of postmodernism, these demonstrable influences show Coetzee to be very much 'of' his intellectual context. The predominantly (though not exclusively) anti-realist orientation of his work also contributes to a sense of inevitability in the application of the label 'postmodernist'. Another reason for this designation is that he belongs to a generation of writers whose exposure to poststructuralist thought is clearly evident in their writing. For academics who are also novelists (like Coetzee), this seems irrefutable.

Even so, Coetzee's ambivalent treatment of poststructuralist ideas also gives us pause, and reminds us that he is elusive of categorization. Mindful of the broader literary-historical context, Attridge challenges the view that Coetzee's work should be labelled 'postmodernist', and proposes either 'late modernism' or 'neomodernism' as more suitable terms: 'Coetzee's work follows on from Kafka and Beckett, not Pynchon and Barth', he writes. Attridge argues against that view of modernism in which the self-reflexive preoccupation with form signals apolitical withdrawal. To the contrary, he presents modernist innovation as having political potential. In this argument, the self-conscious foregrounding of formal devices and the refusal of 'transparent' language as a window on reality are allied to Coetzee's ethical concerns. The logic here is that an innovative mode of expression may have the effect of tacitly rejecting accepted modes of representation, exposing their inadequacy to the task of capturing experience. In making this gesture, modernist expression of the kind developed by Coetzee finds a way of registering the claims of otherness. Attridge finds in Coetzee a reinvigoration of modernist practices, and a related tendency to lay bare both the possibilities and limits of political action. (See Attridge, *J. M. Coetzee and the Ethics of Reading*, pp. 2–6.)

It is possible to see the influence of Samuel Beckett on Coetzee – most especially the prose of Beckett's 'middle' period, *Watt*, *Molloy*, *Malone Dies* and *The Unnameable* – as having a crucial bearing on his technique and the related ethical effects. It is Beckett's exploration of the exhaustion of language, discernible in his obsession with language permutation and word games, that is pertinent here. If this tendency in Beckett reveals an exasperation with the limits of literary language to engage the larger problems of the experience of modernity (including its history and politics), then Coetzee's influence in (and appropriation of) Beckettian concerns may be taken as an index of his desire to take up the modernist dilemma of historical engagement at the level of form. (See the essay by Gilbert Yeoh listed in the section on further reading.)

Echoes of Kafka's work can be found in several of Coetzee's novels, most obviously in the echo of Josef K (the protagonist of Kafka's *The Trial*) in Michael K. Another example is the apparent influence of Kafka's unpleasant story 'In the Penal Colony' on *Waiting for the Barbarians*. (Michael Valdez Moses's essay 'The Mark of Empire: Writing, History, and Torture in Coetzee's *Waiting for the Barbarians*' shows how Kafka's story is refracted through a Foucauldean lens in the novel.) It is the combined sense of nightmare and inscrutable authority in Kafka that Coetzee appropriates, and which resonates powerfully in his treatments of oppression and marginalization. As is typical of Coetzee, however, the question of the influence of Kafka becomes a self-conscious idea in the fiction, most notably at the end of *Elizabeth Costello*, where the echo/parody of Kafka's story/parable 'At the Gate' is the topic of Costello's own bemused reflection (*EC*, p.209). The effect of this is to engage readers in the debate about Coetzee's modernist inheritance.

Another way of expressing Coetzee's various literary allegiances and influences is to say that his work illustrates very well how the 'post' in postmodernism can be quite properly taken to indicate an extension of modernism, as well as a challenge to it, and to the dynamic of modernity. Indeed, without such an understanding, the historical complexity of a writer like Coetzee is difficult to define.

The postmodernism to which Coetzee may be seen to be partly affiliated is based on a notion of hybridity – embracing literary and intellectual identity, as well as his own historical moment – which serves to break down simple binary oppositions, such as modernism/postmodernism, first world/third world. Coetzee contributes to that brand of postcolonial writing in which these oppositions are reconstituted in a more complex transitional model. Coetzee's work corresponds, to some degree, to the 'postcolonial contra-modernity' identified by Homi Bhabha, where a 'postcolonial time-lag' allows the discourses of modernity to be addressed from a postcolonial perspective (*The Location of Culture*, p. 252). This time-lag identifies moments of transition, enabling the writer to explore new political identities in the process of being formed; and Coetzee's novels repeatedly gesture towards new political identities in this way.

There remain to discuss two crucial contextual factors, from the South African political situation, which have a bearing on the modes of Coetzee's fiction. The first, stemming from the ideological control of the apartheid regime, is censorship; the other, from that period of 'interregnum' in the first years of the new South Africa, is the Truth and Reconciliation Commission, the operations of which have influenced Coetzee's thinking about confession.

Censorship is a concern for any South African writer. In the case of Coetzee, none of his novels were banned, although copies of his second novel *In the Heart of the Country* were impounded by customs officials for a while, before the book was allowed to be freely published. Even if he did not fall foul of the apartheid censorship machine, however, censorship has certainly been a preoccupation for him. In *The Master of Petersburg*, for example, the revolutionary ideologue Nechaev is seen effectively censoring the statement written by Coetzee's fictional 'Dostoevsky', and this is indicative of a wider concern for Coetzee. Denying the privacy of the writer, and calling for 'new rules', Nechaev's view invokes the idea of state censorship; and so, through Nechaev, Coetzee establishes the two obstacles for the writer to resist in charting a course: on one side there is the Scylla of ideological conformity; on the other, the Charybdis of state control and censorship.

The literary dimension to the effects of censorship is clear in Coetzee's essay 'Breyten Breytenbach and the Censor' (1991). Coetzee shows how Breytenbach's prison poetry, where the voice of the censor or oppressor is present and contested, can be illuminated with reference to Bakhtin's notion of hidden contestatory dialogue. Such writing generates a form of self-interrogation, in which the self dissolves. Coetzee relates this dissolution to the loss of integrity suffered by the victim of interrogation and torture, in which the victim is tainted with some of the degradation of the persecutor. The consequence of this is to produce a form of doubling of the self, or of 'interrogator and revolutionary, criminal and victim, colonizer and colonized, even censor and writer'. Coetzee's essential point is that, for those caught up in the nets of colonial oppression, in one capacity or another, 'getting to the real self is a life's task' that cannot be accomplished by a simple act of denunciation ('Breyten Breytenbach and the Censor', pp. 94–6).

The moment of doubling, conceived as an effect of censorship, is an integral feature in the movement of decolonization (as a psychological process), since the recognition of contamination is also the instance of confrontation, the point wherein the colonial dynamic is identified, arrested and, potentially, transcended. But the element of contamination can, quite equally, prove disabling, the route to a circular form of self-accusation. This may be another way of accounting for the ambivalence of Coetzee's particular brand of postcolonial expression.

As we saw in chapter 1, Coetzee's interest in the problem of confessional writing can be traced back to the early 1980s and his important essay on this topic, which he has identified as a pivotal moment in his career (*DP*, p. 394). In the next two chapters we will see how the technical problems Coetzee identifies in the confessional mode have been worked through in the novels: *Age of Iron* and *The Master of Petersburg* are particularly relevant here.

This ongoing interest in confession was given a potent point of contextual reference with the establishment of the Truth and Reconciliation Commission (TRC) in 1994. This body was charged with the task of conducting nationwide hearings across South Africa in the hope of bringing to light crimes committed during the apartheid years. The utopian idea behind the TRC was that the transition to a multiracial democracy might be enhanced by bringing together the perpetrators and victims of crimes, and eliciting from them confession and testimony to achieve a form of catharsis.

In practice, the process was often flawed and unsatisfactory. The Commission had the power to grant amnesty to the guilty if it was felt that a full confession had been made, that the whole 'truth' had been established. Yet, for practical reasons, an artificial closure had to be imposed on hearings, with the consequence that the judgement of the Commission – and the justice it dispensed – was sometimes felt to be arbitrary. (Coetzee's depiction of the committee to which David Lurie must confess in *Disgrace* is clearly related to the concerns about the TRC.)

The portrayal of that committee also indicates the author's dismay at the development of a rule-driven, regulated society, and this concern is the most recent pressing contextual issue in Coetzee's work. In particular, there is a preoccupation with how a managerial ethos now governs university life, hampering the academic freedom previously enjoyed by academics. In *Elizabeth Costello* the title character reflects, 'if she were asked to name the core of the university today, its core discipline, she would say it was moneymaking' (*EC*, p. 125). In *Diary of a Bad Year*, the Coetzee figure's mini-essay 'On universities' makes the broader historical context of this concern clear. As a consequence of the threat of funding cuts, through the 1980s and 1990s, universities, JC writes, 'allowed themselves to be turned into business enterprises, in which professors who had previously carried on their enquiries in sovereign freedom were transformed into harried employees required to fulfil quotas under the scrutiny of professional managers'. The possibility of restoring 'the old powers of the professoriat', he suggests, 'is much to be doubted' (*DBY*, p. 35).

Coetzee evidently shares this dismay with his character JC. And what is true of the mechanistic, rule- and target-driven nature of the modern university, underpinned by brute economics, is true of the contemporary world more generally. The resistance of Coetzee now stands in opposition to this regulated society, and the self-interest (in an unequal world) that drives it.

Works I

This chapter considers Coetzee's first six novels, from *Dusklands* (1974) to *Age of Iron* (1990), works written under the shadow of apartheid. In presenting this substantial period of Coetzee's writing as a 'phase' I am implicitly proposing an apartheid/post-apartheid dividing line in his career. While this does not obviously register other complicating elements, which I hope my accounts are sensitive to – the unique creative departure that each novel represents, and yet the continuities to be found through the oeuvre – the dividing line does identify an important shift of emphasis that is becoming clearer with hindsight.

This tentative periodization is, thus, more than a matter of organizational convenience. However, given that one of the main and recurring criticisms of Coetzee's work has been his perceived failure to engage directly with historical and political questions, it might seem surprising to propose this overarching sense of political responsiveness. This is not to suggest an overt degree of response or engagement; but the analyses that follow are based on the premise that Coetzee's fictional preoccupations in his first six novels are profoundly determined by, and permeated with, a consciousness of life in South Africa as a constant and inevitable background presence. In these novels the recurring ideas cannot be fully understood in isolation from that context. Coetzee's imagination, from his earliest work, has been haunted by issues pertaining to mastery/slavery, the colonizing psyche, and the problem of complicity. It is the task of this chapter to outline how these concerns find expression in specifically literary form, through Coetzee's emphasis on textual structures, and his challenge to novelistic conventions.

Dusklands

Dusklands is widely perceived to have introduced a new postmodernist strain in South African fiction: it includes no mimetic representation of its contemporary context, but makes the question of discourse its focus. Announcing the typical Coetzean style, with its emphasis on textuality, the modus operandi of *Dusklands* is to interrogate particular narrative modes. Superficially, this is a straightforward business, since Coetzee chooses two instances of imperialist discourse and subjects them to parodic treatment. Yet there is also a strand of reflexive self-critique in the parody, and this serves to question, implicitly, the austere nature of postmodernist expression. We are invited to reflect on the absence of overt judgement about the horrors of imperialism that the novel treats: here, as in much of his work, Coetzee pre-empts his critics, anticipating the charge of moral failure. The effect of this self-critique, however, is to suggest an incipient, if fastidious, ethical stance.

The novel is divided into two novellas; but since the whole is dependent on the interrelationship of these two narratives – for example, through the development of theme and motif – the book is clearly a unified and single entity. The first section, 'The Vietnam Project', traces its narrator's progression into insanity, as the discourse of US imperialism overwhelms him. Eugene Dawn is writing a report for the US Defense Department about the psychological war in Vietnam, a form of discourse – parodied in one subsection – partially dignified by a pseudo-rationality that only serves to heighten the impression of a kind of madness lurking beneath the surface of things. (Coetzee's point of reference is a collection of Hudson Institute reports, *Can We Win in Vietnam?* (1968), from which the novel's epigraph is taken.)

The second section, 'The Narrative of Jacobus Coetzee', is based on the colonial travel writing of European adventurers in the Cape in the seventeenth and eighteenth centuries; and the fact that the original Jacobus Coetsé was a distant relative of the author adds great resonance to the theme of complicity in this novel. These two narratives invite readers to draw parallels between contemporary US imperialism in Vietnam and the historical origin of Afrikaner domination in South Africa; embedded in this parallel, and the modes of discourse Coetzee appropriates, is a debate about authorial power and complicity, which, through historical association, is rendered personal for Coetzee.

Dusklands has been criticized for its oblique method, and for failing to offer a clearer moral perspective on the colonial violence it depicts. Critics have even wondered if it serves to reproduce a colonial form of aggressive self-aggrandizement. It is important, however, to remember that complicity is a central theme of the novel, and is investigated through the two extraordinary narrators, Eugene Dawn and Jacobus Coetzee. Yet, in the absence of overt authorial judgement, Coetzee has recourse to less obvious devices to expose colonialism. Irony is the principal tool here, and critics have disagreed as to whether or not the ironic undercutting is extensive enough to treat appropriately the kind of brutality that Coetzee describes; or, indeed, if irony is a sharp enough tool for the job. The irony is certainly pervasive, and is reinforced by the book's structure and the effects Coetzee generates through pattern and juxtaposition. Some of the violent scenes are uncomfortable, and some readers will continue to be repelled by the book; but that may also be part of the purpose of a work that is deliberately discomfiting. (It is interesting to note, however, that Coetzee became more cautious in his treatment of violence in subsequent works, notably *Waiting for the Barbarians*, *Disgrace* and *Elizabeth Costello*.)

The second section, 'The Narrative of Jacobus Coetzee', is the longer of the two, and this is where the book's emphasis lies: the treatment of US policy in Vietnam then serves as a prelude to the longer account of Dutch colonial activities in eighteenth-century South Africa. 'The Vietnam Project' introduces themes, attitudes and key terms that are developed in 'The Narrative of Jacobus Coetzee', and which gather significance through the cumulative process of reading.

In 'The Vietnam Project', the insanity of Eugene Dawn stems from his work as a mythographer for the US military. One of the dehumanizing effects of war is shown to stem from the assertion of racial and cultural difference in the prosecution of military tactics. Dawn's psychological collapse stems from this, a collapse that culminates in the scene where he kidnaps and stabs his son. Coetzee is targeting a broad concept of patriarchy, which uncovers an allegorical association between Dawn and the USA: the paternal imperialism of the USA reveals it to be an 'unnatural father', too.

The critique of patriarchy also implicates an aggressive form of male sexuality, in which the other is reduced to an object of exploitation and violence. Coetzee conducts a debate about the pornographic imagination through a series of photographs of war atrocities, with which Dawn is obsessed, and which his wife blames for the change in his mental state (*D*, p. 10). One of these may be an image of child rape (*D*, p. 13). Another, a still from a propaganda film of caged prisoners, is Dawn's particular fascination. The still freezes the moment before the imprisoned man's fearful glance meets the camera. Haunted by the glint in the eye of the imprisoned man, he runs his fingers fetishistically over the surface of the print, hoping to make the image of the man 'yield' its 'interior'. (Dawn is occupied thus since 'evenings are quiet here in the suburbs' (*D*, pp. 16–17).)

This desire, which plainly parallels the penetrative (yet paradoxical) desire of colonial domination, is channelled through a form of technological control. Coetzee here links technology, US imperialism and the experience of postmodernity – a prescient idea for 1974, even if it is more familiar now. (*In Postmodernism, or, the Cultural Logic of Late Capitalism*, Fredric Jameson situates the Vietnam War in just this kind of historical phase.) Dawn's fantasy of control or penetration, on quiet evenings in the suburbs, anticipates what is now a commonplace idea in American culture: that beneath the social mores of suburbia there seethes a tide of latent violence.

There is an important paradox in Dawn's film still: there is frustration in the fact that the image will not 'yield' its 'interior'; yet it is the arrested moment before the fearful prisoner faces the camera that makes it so fascinating for him. This paradox is developed in Dawn's account of US aggression in Vietnam, justified as the desire to find someone to stand up to the bullets: 'if you will prove yourself, we shouted, you will prove us too' (*D*, p. 17). The idea that imperial violence is a desperate quest for ontological reassurance becomes central to the psychological profile of Jacobus Coetzee.

The insecurity of the colonizer produces a series of contradictory self-projections. This insecurity lies behind the cultural imperialism of Jacobus Coetzee, and his failure to understand or appreciate indigenous culture, as when he is distressed by the Namaqua dance he observes. He perceives the dance to be an imitation of the courtship ritual of the dove, and the reader may imagine a certain dignity and humour in the different aspects of sexuality implied in the dance; yet Jacobus is made anxious by the patterns of the dance which make him wish that the dancers would 'drop their pantomime and cavort in an honest sexual frenzy culminating in mass coitus' (*D*, p. 86). The phallocentric view carries with it the desire to debase, and control, other forms of cultural expression.

Jacobus's barbarism is the result of his solipsism, philistinism and phallocentric aggression. When he is reduced to leading a Bushman's life (as he imagines it), the inversion of the roles of 'master' and 'savage', on which this narrative is predicated, is underscored. Like Eugene Dawn, Jacobus Coetzee articulates the colonial project as a (plainly illogical) quest for ontological reassurance. Ridiculed on his first expedition to 'the land of the Great Namaqua', Jacobus undertakes a second, vengeful expedition to the Namaqua village, the scene of his humiliation, and it is here that the most extreme violence of the book occurs. These descriptions are unpleasant because they are narrated from Jacobus's deranged perspective; but they do reveal the essential insecurity of the colonizer's psyche. The Namaqua village is razed to the ground, its inhabitants raped and slaughtered, and Jacobus articulates his actions as an assertion of his reality, invoking the inscrutability of divine judgement. Yet he also presents himself as 'a tool in the hands of history'; he is part of a broader colonial history, we understand, an idea that implicates a broader notion of the white man's volition in the violence over which Jacobus presides (*D*, p. 106).

In some respects, it is hard to situate this novel within the broader field of postcolonialism, since its power (and horror) resides in the vivid imagining of colonial violence, even though Coetzee works hard to undermine the perspective that gives rise to such imaginings. There are, however, moments that point more obviously beyond the colonial frame, and which reveal Jacobus to be Coetzee's construct, implicitly aware of his contradictory position. At one moment, for example, Jacobus envisages his faithful servant Klawer turning the tables on him: 'he threatens to have a history in which I shall be a term. Such is the material basis of the malady of the master's soul' (*D*, p. 81). If we can take Klawer to represent the colonized other, then his latent power of assertion, figured as the possession of a history, is an anticipation of the postcolonial world.

An indication of the contemporary relevance of *Dusklands* can be gleaned from Coetzee's later essay, 'Idleness in South Africa' (1982) (*WW*, pp. 12–35). A focus of this essay is the perspective of European travellers from the seventeenth century, and their accounts of the Khoi people of the Cape – 'Hottentots' as they were called. These accounts express horror and disgust at the Hottentot way of life, and especially at the perceived idleness. Coetzee ascribes to the eye of the European colonizer a limited structural anthropology that was bound to misrepresent the codes of Hottentot society. Such travel writers – among them the first Afrikaner settlers – superimposed their own grid of behavioural expectations, against which the perception of Hottentot idleness seemed scandalous. Coetzee's point is that the Hottentot frustrated the colonizer's desire to write their accounts, failing to supply the traveller-writer with useful data (*WW*, p. 23). The analytical eye of these travellers, determined by that grid of expectations, embodied a form of imperialism at the level of discourse, the desire to assimilate indigenous African culture to European codes of explanation. The European's disappointment when confronted with Hottentot idleness finds an equivalent in *Dusklands* in the colonizer's dismay when he encounters no native capable of standing up to his violent probes. In both cases, it is the certainty of European identity that is shaken, and this further demonstrates the postcolonial credentials of Coetzee's first novel. When the travellers consider the sequence of daily events, Hottentot life is shown to be far from idle, being taken up with all manner of societal business – involving intrigue and surveillance, as well as the more mundane matters of subsistence.

'Idleness in South Africa' ends with a consideration of the apartheid era, and this signals quite clearly the contemporary political relevance of *Dusklands*. Coetzee considers some of the central planks of early apartheid legislation – the Immorality Act (1950) and the Mixed Marriages Act (1949) – speculating that these cornerstones of racial separation (which outlawed interracial relationships) may have been motivated by the same kind of impulse that provoked disgust in those early European travellers, the fear that white working men might be tempted to settle down to idle lives with 'brown women', spawning large, unproductive families. This speculation about the social engineering of apartheid suggests that the persisting fantasy of native idleness was at its root.

The text of *Dusklands* contains the same kind of historical bridge, most clearly in the circumstances surrounding S. J. Coetzee, the 'editor' of Jacobus's narrative, who, we are told, conducted work between 1934 and 1948 on the early explorers of South Africa. This was the period when the mythology of apartheid was fashioned, drawing on a Nationalist idea of the Afrikaner pioneering spirit. The connection is emphasized in the 'Afterword', where S. J. Coetzee emulates something of the contradictory pseudo-rationality that characterizes the perspective of Jacobus.

It is important that the larger historical and political frame for the novel is signalled by another 'Coetzee'. Yet *another* Coetzee in the novel is Eugene Dawn's shadowy supervisor, and he shares a position of withdrawal with Dawn's other 'supervisor', the novelist who created him. The proliferation of 'Coetzees' in the novel clearly flags up its metafictional procedures, the emphasis on the examination of narrative modes, and the impulses behind them. More important, perhaps, is how the author's sense of complicity is emphasized by all those Coetzees. This complicity has partly to do with Coetzee's far from radical position as a professional intellectual in South Africa, importing the Western codes of poststructuralism and avant-garde literary expression into his country's literature; but it has also to do with his historical affiliation, the ancestry that implicates him in the early colonial discourse of the Cape. However, it is that sense of complicity, clearly acknowledged, that opens up the ethical space that justifies the writing of a book like *Dusklands*, as Coetzee has himself observed (*DP*, p. 343).

In the Heart of the Country

Coetzee's second novel, *In the Heart of the Country* (1977), is, if anything, more difficult and forbidding than his first. As with much of his work, this novel betrays an anxiety about the role of the intellectual/writer in South Africa. There are also important reflections on Afrikaner mythology, and on the South African literary tradition, in a disruptive narrative presented as a series of 266 numbered sections. Written at a time of increasing international isolation for South Africa, this is an inward-looking novel, a point emphasized by the South African edition, in which the dialogue was written in Afrikaans.

The novel is presented as a first-person monologue, or perhaps as a kind of journal, in which the speaker, Magda, emerges as the symbolic daughter of colonialism. As always with Coetzee, there is both an intellectual and a historical aspect to the treatment of colonialism. A feature of the novel, which contributes to its inward-looking character, is that the distinction between imagination and event is blurred – most obviously when we read contradictory accounts of events. We learn to focus on the construction of Magda's narrative, and what this reveals about her. She tells of her father's new (and apparently imaginary) new bride, and of her brutal murder of the newlyweds, with an axe (*IHC*, p. 11), though the father appears to be alive and well soon after this in the narrative (*IHC*, p. 16). In another scenario of patricide, she recounts her father's seduction of 'Klein-Anna', the wife of the black servant Hendrik, and the shooting of her father while he is in bed with his new mistress. After the father is buried, the allegorical connotations of the novel come to the fore. Magda tries, but fails, to establish a rapport with Hendrik and Anna, and she is eventually overrun in her colonial outpost: she is raped and humiliated by Hendrik, and he and Anna eventually abandon her. Deserted on the farm, Magda seems to receive portentous messages about the colonial relationship from machines, or 'sky gods' in the air. The novel closes with some lyrical sections, the father now alive again, as Magda offers a form of nostalgic celebration of an older rural existence.

The important thing to grasp about Magda's unstable interior monologue is that it enacts the psychological confusions and divisions of the colonial mindset, in an extension of Coetzee's concerns in *Dusklands*. The development apparent in *In the Heart of the Country* is that Magda occupies an ambivalent position, as both victim and perpetrator of colonialism.

The landscape is crucial to the way Coetzee yokes together the different aspects of colonialism, historical, psychological and intellectual. The remote veld where the farm is located is a space resistant to colonial organization, a place where family relations, labour relations and sexual relations become disastrously confused, in a microcosm of the social contradictions produced by the exercise of colonial power. As we shall see, Coetzee links this with his literary project of writing back to the pastoral tradition in the South African novel. The historical location is imprecise: the forms of transport used (horse, bicycle, train) suggest a farm of the late nineteenth or early twentieth century; yet such details as the appearance of aeroplanes at the end of the book bring us into the later twentieth century. As in *Dusklands*, Coetzee creates a fluid sense of the historical context upon which the novel is brought to bear, thus enabling his readers to make connections between the contemporary political situation in South Africa and a longer view of Afrikaner identity.

The inward-looking aspect of the novel might seem to encourage a straightforward allegorical interpretation, in which the spinster Magda stands for South Africa in its international political isolation. Given the conflict between Magda and the servants, we might also detect an allegory of South Africa on the brink of revolution, with Coetzee offering some cautionary thoughts about the retributive use of power. When Hendrik puts on the 'master's' garb, or inverts the mistress/slave relationship in his dealings with Magda, we might detect an allegory of violent political change. These two allegorical patterns do not quite 'line up', however; and this is indicative of Coetzee's deliberate problematizing of allegory, using it as a mode of interpretation itself, in order to unsettle simple correspondences.

Perhaps the most resonant motif in the book is the recurring image of the body being inhabited by the body of another. At one point, Magda, in a reflection on her place in the power relations that surround her, imagines 'the law' standing 'fullgrown inside my shell', with 'its sex drooping through my hole'. She imagines the law gnawing through her, leaving her 'sloughed, crumpled, abandoned on the floor' (*IHC*, p. 84). To the extent that the law is the law of language and command, Magda both possesses and is possessed by it. Yet the personification of the law as male, and as a parasite devouring Magda's body, emphasizes the partly colonized position of the white woman in colonial structures, obliged to support a model of power to which her own identity is subordinated. Magda presents this phallocentrism as a form of rape from within. After the sections describing Hendrik's rape of her, Magda wonders if he is plotting to take over her body by cramming his frame within hers (*IHC*, p. 108), a fear that encapsulates Magda's embattled position as female in the impending postcolonial power struggle.

Magda, too, expresses the desire to inhabit another, in this case Anna, Hendrik's wife (*IHC*, pp. 108–9). This implicates Magda in the motif of invasion and possession; but there are positive connotations, too. The desire to inhabit Anna's body enables her to imagine herself as Hendrik's sexual partner in other circumstances, thus confounding the psychological wrong of Hendrik's sexual violence. She also imagines herself experiencing the veld with Anna's sensory perceptions, clearly expressing the wish to open herself to alternative cultural representations of the land.

Coetzee's principle of composition in the novel is to place emphasis on the construction of identity. As Magda puts it, 'I make it all up in order that it shall make me up' (*IHC*, p. 73). The uncertainty of the status of events in the novel orients us towards this psychological focus. In a sense, the construction of Magda becomes a textual problem, since her narrative is a fabric shot through with quotations from, or allusions to, modern European writers and philosophers, including Blake, Hegel, Kierkegaard, Freud, Kafka, Sartre and Beckett. Her discourse is also influenced by literary theory, a point that lays bare her status as a metafictional device, facilitating Coetzee's exploration of how character is constructed, and his self-conscious preoccupation with the 'I-figure' in narrative fiction. This more theoretical, metafictional aspect of the book is given a vital, contextual dimension by being attached to Coetzee's subversion of the pastoral tradition in the South African novel.

In his essay 'Farm Novel and Plaasroman' (*WW*, pp. 63–81), Coetzee makes the case for an antipastoral tradition in the English-language novel of South African farm life, a tradition clearly continued by *In the Heart of the Country*. The essay considers the antipastoralism of Oliver Schreiner, and the idealistic pastoral of Pauline Smith; and, in the light of the essay, we can say that Coetzee's novel extends – considerably extends – the antipastoral vision of Schreiner, whilst seeking to identify the social gaps evident in Smith's idealized pastoral idyll. Coetzee considers Schreiner's *Story of an African Farm* to be a 'microcosm of colonial South Africa' (*WW*, p. 65), and we can read *In the Heart of the Country* as a pointed updating of that microcosmic view. He also observes the silence, in the South African pastoral idyll, about the place of the black man (*WW*, p. 81). The prominence of Hendrik and Anna in Coetzee's novel addresses this literary-historical omission.

When Magda asserts that her medium of writing is lyric rather than chronicle, she draws our attention to an important aspect of the novel, and, indeed, of Coetzee's writing more generally: in a complex sense, lyric rather than chronicle is his medium (*IHC*, p. 71). Coetzee's lyricism develops through the oeuvre, and is tailored to specific contexts and precise discursive interventions. Here, Magda's lyricism, especially towards the end of the novel, is an integral feature of the novel's antipastoralism. Magda's lyricism becomes a form of circular nostalgia, the mode that conveys her desire to recuperate the old pastoral dream of white independence. Earlier in the book, however, we have been alerted to the problematic nature of Magda's lyricism, since it appears in certain purple passages where it is disturbingly misdirected.

One example is her account of how her father should have died, while the corpse lies 'black with his heavy blood' after her act of patricide: 'it would have been better for him to have yielded the gentle ghost, following it as far as he could on its passage out, closing his eyes on the image of a swallow swooping, rising, riding' (*IHC*, pp. 14–15). Such passages train the reader to be wary of Magda's lyricism, and to be alert to the disjunction between the celebratory (and sometimes clichéd) poetic form and the brutal content it overlays. By using lyricism against itself in this way, Coetzee manages, paradoxically, to produce a form of consonance through the dissonance: in this instance, the imagined death of the father, who is the quintessential Afrikaner patriarch, is appropriately associated with the 'dying fall' of the mode of pastoral lyricism, with its ideological bad faith exposed.

There is a sequence in the final pages where Magda claims to be addressed by voices speaking in Spanish, coming from flying machines overhead. These voices are associated with a utopian future of universal meanings, evoking the unifying idealism of Esperanto (Magda understands the voices, even though she knows no Spanish) (*IHC*, p. 126). For these voices, Coetzee draws on Sartre and Hegel, and a tradition of philosophy in which the dialectic of self and other, and the bond of the master and slave, are articulated. These are messages that imply some of the intellectual foundations of postcolonial theory and, in turning away from these messages, Magda fails to comprehend their full significance, and the nature of her predicament as a symbolic late colonial agent.

What she turns to is a gesture of ambivalent lyricism, a studiedly nostalgic withdrawal which, in the final section of the book, emerges as a kind of prop for an Afrikaner identity in need of reconstruction. Her conscious embrace of a 'nostalgia for country ways', now she is alone – and racially apart, abandoned by 'the ghostly brown figures' – is an acknowledged failure in social terms. In this sense, her 'closing plangencies' are genuinely mournful, whilst simultaneously self-ironizing (*IHC*, p. 139).

In his Jerusalem Prize acceptance speech (1987), Coetzee traces the false self/other opposition of apartheid back to the misdirected passion of the early colonizers. The 'love' of the 'hereditary masters of South Africa', he suggests, 'has consistently been directed toward *the land*, that is, toward what is least likely to respond to love: mountains and deserts, birds and animals and flowers'. This 'failure of love' corresponds with Magda's final pastoral nostalgia, which emulates the misplaced love of the 'masters' of South Africa as her celebration of the landscape and its wildlife supplants her efforts towards fraternity (*DP*, p. 97).

Yet fraternity is what Magda has craved; but in the end she finds herself contained in a literary genre (pastoral) which does not allow her passion an outlet. The antipastoralism of *In the Heart of the Country* is rooted in this tension. Magda strives for fraternity, through her overtures to Anna and Hendrik, but is defeated by the constraints of genre, which re-channel her passion towards an unregenerated pastoral vision, or, the wrong kind of love.

The self-conscious and inward-looking nature of this book reveals an anxiety on the author's part about what is happening to literature in South Africa. The circularity of Magda's narrative suggests the possibility of a dead end, an imaginative failure, illustrated by Magda's misguided lyricism which relies upon the pastoral mode that it also subverts. Coetzee's recourse to Beckett, as a prominent European literary model in this novel, implies his own concerns about the possibilities for creativity in South African litera-ture, and an anxiety about the role of the kind of postmodernism he is pioneering. There is one telling moment where Magda seems to reject the philosophical abstractions of Beckett, and to make a direct appeal to the Real, and to an end-orientated version of history (*IHC*, pp. 119–20). Even so, there is something resigned about the defiance, which simultaneously reveals Magda's intellectual provenance, and so reaffirms her textual prison: she is an artificial postmodernist phenomenon, a character familiar with *Happy Days*, and with Beckett's obsession with permutation. To this extent, Coetzee's literary self-consciousness reveals his own anxiety about an inheritance that seems barren.

This is not to suggest that the presence of European influences in African literature is a demonstrable instance of cultural imperialism. Coetzee is aware that his work is open to such simplistic charges, and one of his great achievements is to work through and beyond that kind of critique. In the case of *In the Heart of the Country*, the authority of the work stems from its allusiveness. An important example is the reference to Hegel's work on the master/slave, or lord/bondsman dialectic. Teresa Dovey has shown that Magda translates a key section from Hegel's *Phenomenology of Spirit* con-cerning the paradoxical bond between lord and bondsman (*IHC*, p. 130). (See *The Novels of J. M. Coetzee*, p. 23.) Hegel argues that the lord's position of mastery depends on the self-consciousness of the bondsman, which means that the lord cannot have the independent status that the self-consciousness of his own position necessitates. It is the bondsman, therefore, who occupies a position of genuine self-consciousness, rather than the lord. (See Hegel, *Phenomenology of Spirit*, pp. 116–17.)

This idea, that the lord/bondsman relationship reveals an inverse authenticity that validates the bondsman, is a background presence throughout the novel; and it speaks to Coetzee's metafictional project as much as it does to the action of the novel. The model of decolonization that might flow from the idea of inverse authenticity is suggestive of the need for a form of literary hybridity, a mode of writing in which the post-colonizer's intellectual inheritance can be both utilized and interrogated at the same time. That intellectual inheritance is then authenticated through the process of being deployed to reveal the anterior authenticity of the oppressed other, though this may involve the uncovering of different degrees of oppression in a hierarchy of control. Such a mode of writing, with just these effects, is precisely what Coetzee achieves in *In the Heart of the Country*.

Waiting for the Barbarians

The topic of complicity, articulated through instances of historical and intellectual affiliation in the first two novels, reaches a new plateau of self-confrontation in *Waiting for the Barbarians* (1980). The idea of personal awakening – that which is ultimately out of reach for Magda in the previous novel – now becomes a decisive structural principle.

Waiting for the Barbarians encapsulates the central problem for readers of Coetzee's writing in the apartheid era, since it seems simultaneously to engage with, and yet distance itself from, its political context. There are obvious parallels with apartheid South Africa in 1980 in a novel about a man of conscience seeking to disentangle himself from, and oppose, an imperial regime: this might be taken to establish an archetype of white resistance. Yet the vagueness of the setting, with regard to both time and place, lends the book the air of a universal allegory of imperialism. There are still specific details, however, that clearly resonate with contemporaneous concerns in South Africa. The overall effect is typical of postmodernist allegory, a mode that both develops and questions the allegorizing impulse.

The focus of the novel is a walled town, a frontier outpost of 'Empire'. The omission of the definite article is one of the features that help cultivate the air of a universal allegory: 'Empire' seems to represent imperialism *per se*. The novel's narrator is the magistrate of the settlement, and it is his process of awakening – a painful and ambivalent process – that allows a deep understanding of imperialism to emerge. The magistrate's own sense of complicity is the key to this, and a vital aspect of the novel's ethical stance.

Certain codes of realism are more evident in this novel than in the previous two, producing a more conventional narrative chronology, descriptive style and narrative voice. Yet the strain of postmodernist questioning and ambiguity persists, making this a typically problematic work in which different traditions are put into a dialectical relationship, from which a synthesis – embodying a new postcolonial ethic – might emerge.

The settlement is at the frontier of the Empire's domain; beyond this point lies territory inhabited by the nomadic barbarians. The novel opens with the arrival of Colonel Joll and his men from Empire's Third Bureau, and the commencement of their operations to deal with a perceived barbarian threat. Joll presides over a regime of terror, involving interrogation and torture, and the directive to discover the 'truth' predetermined by Empire's Manichean ethos. This is the base imperial drive for self-assertion, satisfied by the subjugation of those who are identified as the barbarian other.

The magistrate develops an ambivalent interest in one of the torture victims, a young 'barbarian' girl who has been nearly blinded, and whose ankles, broken by her torturers, are now deformed. Through his relationship with the girl, the magistrate recognizes his affinities with her torturers, and begins his journey of self-discovery. He undertakes an expedition to return her to her own people, but is branded a collaborator on his return, and is himself subjected to torture and humiliation. At the end of the novel, the settlement is abandoned by the Third Bureau garrison, their mission sabotaged by the tactics and stealth of the elusive nomadic people. Many citizens have fled, and a reduced population remains, waiting for the barbarians.

Coetzee takes his title from the poem of the same name by the Greek poet, C. P. Cavafy (1863–1933). Cavafy's poem presents the Roman Empire, decadent, precarious, awaiting the arrival of 'the barbarians' who will take over the machinery of government. This 'waiting' is an anticipation of the imperialist self-prophecy, a form of justification that is also self-negation: the imperialist project is based on the perception of the barbarian other, and the anticipation of the eventual succession of this other. In the poem, the barbarians fail to arrive – they cease to exist – and no longer embody 'a kind of solution'. Cavafy's poem identifies the contradictory dependence on the other that underpins imperialism; and it is this idea, already evident in Coetzee's two previous novels, that clearly chimes with *Waiting for the Barbarians*.

While Colonel Joll is waiting for the barbarian other, however, the magistrate has been waiting for a different manifestation of barbarism. Where Joll, like the Romans in Cavafy's poem, needs to discover barbarians to validate his mission and the existence of Empire, the magistrate finds barbarism in the activities of Joll and his garrison: for him, the waiting has been for the true nature of Empire to be revealed; and, following the revelation, he begins the difficult process of disentangling himself from its ideological control.

In the magistrate's plight, it is impossible not to see an allegory of the South African liberal, at the time of the book's composition, coming to terms with the fact of privilege in, and complicity with the apartheid system. The novel is typical of Coetzee, however, in refusing the kind of detailed correspondences that are found in a sustained political allegory. The result is an unsettling mode that falls somewhere between a universal allegory or parable about power and oppression, and an excoriating critique of a specific form of oppression. On the one hand, it is impossible not to agree with David Attwell, that Coetzee's Empire is a parody of the apartheid regime, in its paranoia and attempted control of history (*J. M. Coetzee*, pp. 73–4); yet the vagueness of the setting enables the book to elude its context as well, to achieve that form of rivalry with history that is so important to Coetzee.

The political resonances were certainly clear for contemporary readers. In the novel, the sense of guilt and fear of those abandoning the settlement clearly parallels the actions of those white South Africans who chose to emigrate in the 1970s and 1980s and take up professional careers in other countries. As Susan Gallagher has observed, the emphasis on torture in the novel also clearly evokes the operations of the South African regime following the Soweto riots in 1976–7, especially the killing of Steve Biko while in custody in 1977. (*A Story of South Africa*, chapter 5.)

Torture in *Waiting for the Barbarians* is also a textual matter, however. This becomes clear in the scene where the word 'ENEMY' is written in charcoal on the backs of a line of barbarian prisoners, who are then thrashed until the word cannot be read (*WB*, pp. 104–6). Coetzee is alluding to Kafka's story 'In the Penal Colony', here, a brutal story in which inscription and execution are conjoined in a deluded notion of justice. In Kafka's story, the inscription on the back of a condemned prisoner is revealed to be a self-destructive expression of power; Coetzee reorients the element of self-defeat to make it refer more directly to the Manichean difference upon which Empire depends, but which is ironically purged when the charcoal inscriptions on the prisoners' backs are beaten away.

Writing retrospectively in his 1986 essay, 'Into the Dark Chamber: the Writer and the South African State', Coetzee describes *Waiting for the Barbarians* as a novel about torture, and the impact of torture on the 'man of conscience'. Coetzee sees torture as presenting a particular dilemma for the

South African novelist, who may fail either by ignoring it, or by reproducing it in some measure through the process of representation. The writer's duty is then 'to establish one's own authority . . . to imagine torture and death on one's own terms'. Again, Coetzee is after that form of rivalry that signals a refusal 'to play the game by the rules of the state', and *Waiting for the Barbarians* can be read as an extended response to this dilemma (*DP*, p. 364).

The dilemma is treated discursively in the novel, in fact – for example, when the magistrate ponders how Joll was initiated as a torturer, and how he manages to return from this activity and 'break bread with other men' (*WB*, p. 12). The magistrate later betrays the same wondering bewilderment when questioning his own torturer, Mandel: 'I am trying to imagine how you breathe and eat and live from day to day. But I cannot!' The questioning insists that the torturer's role is incomprehensible; it also provokes an outburst of genuine violence, revealing the psychological damage done to Mandel (*WB*, p. 126).

The torture endured by the magistrate includes a public beating, being forced to drink pints of brine, and a mock-hanging that nearly strangles him. Unlike the barbarians, however, the magistrate is not being tortured for information: the purpose, as he puts it, is 'to show me the meaning of humanity'. The grim lesson the magistrate is being taught is that high-minded notions of justice can be entertained by the body 'only as long as it is whole and well' (*WB*, p. 115); and the corollary of this is that enduring principles – principles underwritten by the requisite degree of 'humanity' – have to pass the test of personal suffering in some circumstances.

Does this depiction of torture court the danger outlined by Coetzee in 'Into the Dark Chamber', the danger of perpetuating fear and replicating the effect of state violence? Certainly, Coetzee runs this risk; but he seeks to circumvent it. He does this, first by showing that the magistrate does not lose his developing sense of principle, and second because the victim in this instance is also the narrator. This means that the magistrate cannot be rendered as a dehumanized object through an external view: the torturer's perspective, in other words, is not reproduced.

Neither does the unsettling affinity between the magistrate and Joll have the effect of engaging with, or seeming to reproduce, the activities of the oppressor. On the contrary, by having his character worry away at the problem of affinity, Coetzee ensures that the oppressor is not demonised in such a way as to mythologize his power. Rather, the writing strategies Coetzee employs serve to demythologise Empire.

Perceptions of language are foregrounded in the novel. Joll's brutal form of control, for example, is underpinned by a reductive perception of language: he explains to the magistrate how, in the torture chamber, 'a certain tone enters the voice of a man who is telling the truth' (*WB*, p. 5). Initially, the magistrate assumes Joll must have an ear that is remarkably sensitive to linguistic inflection; but his purpose is to reduce all inflection to the single tone of pain/truth, in the same way that the colonizer always tends to destroy indigenous culture, including indigenous language. At one point, the presence of indigenous language is taken as a sign of guilt: some of Joll's first prisoners turn out to be fisherfolk, rather than 'barbarians', arrested by soldiers who could not understand their speech: otherness, denoted by language, is a threat to be neutralized (*WB*, p. 18).

It is through language that the magistrate is most clearly implicated in the mindset of Empire, especially in his relationship with the barbarian girl, which is hampered because they lack a common tongue. When the magistrate hears the girl talking fluently in the pidgin language of the frontier, on the expedition to reunite her with her people, he realizes that she is 'a witty, attractive young woman'; and he regrets not having asked her to teach him this language (*WB*, pp. 63, 71–2). She has been bound to remain inscrutable to him, her alien otherness affirmed through his lack of interest in her language.

The magistrate's ambivalent interest in the barbarian girl is the key to the process of recognizing his affinity with Empire, and distancing himself from it. The magistrate recognizes an affinity with the girl's torturers early on, stemming from a shared fascination with the girl's body as object (*WB*, pp. 27–8). Sexual intercourse occurs between them only once, however, and this is on the expedition, when she is to be freed from the control of Empire, and can make her own choice. Earlier, the magistrate's straightforward phallic desire for the 'bird-like' woman at the inn/brothel is contrasted with his more mysterious desire for the girl. In this mood, he realizes that his urge to find and possess the 'interior' of the girl is a 'mistake', which would be analogous to the ways in which her torturers had marked her 'surface', leaving her crippled and partially blind (*WB*, p. 43). The girl, in fact, is established as a text, and the magistrate cannot give her up until the marks on her body are 'deciphered and understood' (*WB*, p. 31).

It is important to note that these marks, the outward signs of torture, are an aspect of the girl's mystery and her identity. This is to become a telling and recurring idea in Coetzee's fiction: that the force of the colonizer is formative of the identity of the colonized, something to be embraced, a text that forms part of an alternative story that will oppose colonial history. By establishing the girl as a text, Coetzee finds a compelling way to link individual experience to broader questions concerning discourse and power.

A related idea in the novel is revealed in those episodes featuring the wooden slips bearing an ancient script. The magistrate has discovered these slips – of which there are 256, a 'perfect' number – on an archaeological site near to the settlement. He speculates that they may be evidence of a previous outpost, and he is much preoccupied in trying to interpret the script written on them, much as he desires to penetrate the surface of the girl (*WB*, pp. 15–16). When Joll questions him about these slips, he learns the lesson that it is necessary to resist the urge to impose a single meaning. For Joll, the ambiguity is intolerable, suggestive of a hidden code contained in the ancient script, through which the magistrate communicates with the enemy.

Joll's evident desire to make this archaeological phenomenon conform to a frame of interpretation he understands reveals another important allegorical nudge to the reader, evoking the way in which apartheid mythology, rooted in 'settler' history, had been profoundly shaken by archaeological discoveries demonstrating an indigenous African prehistory. The magistrate responds sarcastically to Joll's request for a translation of the scripts: although he has no knowledge of how to read them, he suggests that one depicts the barbarian character 'war', which has other senses, including 'vengeance' and 'justice', depending on which way up it is. Taken together, he proposes, the slips 'form an allegory', and can be read as 'a domestic journal', or 'a plan of war', or 'a history of the last years of the Empire – the old Empire' (*WB*, p. 112).

The lesson the magistrate seems to have learned concerns the fluidity of language, and its nuances, which are lost in a reductive pursuit of a single meaning. The idea of an allegory is typically ambivalent, since Joll's eventual dismissal of the slips as gambling sticks reveals a failure to understand the other that is symptomatic of the failure that will surely signal the history of the end of the current Empire (*WB*, p. 113). His inability to accept the sticks unless they can be reduced to a code of meaning he understands emulates Empire's failure to understand the guerrilla tactics of the barbarians: the Empire's forces are depleted without being able to confront the enemy, because they have imposed their own template of warfare on the confrontation. Yet, if there is an allegorical hint in Joll's dismissal of the sticks, their function, elusive of meaning, is also to undermine the idea of traditional allegory, with its one-to-one correspondence. That form of template clearly conforms to the allegorizing impulse in imperialism, and embodied in Joll: it is this impulse that the novel serves to unsettle.

The ambivalent treatment of allegory is one of the ways in which *Waiting for the Barbarians* investigates and exposes how fiction colludes with representations of history. Another strand to this, as in *In the Heart of the Country*, concerns literary pastoral. The action of *Waiting for the Barbarians*, in accordance with the basic structural principle of pastoral, spans a single year; but, as Attwell points out, here the single seasonal cycle seems a 'flagrantly formal, conventionalised device' where symbolic correspondences between the action and the seasons are revealed as misleading signs (*J. M. Coetzee*, p. 86). Yet there is ambivalence here, too. The signs of spring that appear after the magistrate's expedition to return the barbarian girl are ironic in preceding his arrest and torture (*WB*, p. 76); but they do also herald his sense of elation at feeling himself to have broken his bond with Empire (*WB*, p. 78). Although his sense of freedom is surely premature – there is no clear break from the imprisoning ideology – there are signs of development that suggest the 'springtime' of personal growth.

At the end of the novel, the magistrate sets about writing a history of his experiences, and he finds himself writing a form of pastoral, celebrating his time in the 'oasis' of his town. He dismisses this history at once, however, as 'devious', 'equivocal' and 'reprehensible'. (This repeats his earlier abortive attempt to begin a history.) Desiring to escape the history that Empire has imposed, he feels this must involve living 'outside history' (*WB*, p. 154). This introduces the idea of an alternative framework for history, an alternative form of narrative, even though the magistrate does not seem well placed to realize such a narrative.

The magistrate's (failed) attempt at pastoral is another convention, and cannot be usefully pitted against the Empire's teleological and apocalyptic version of history (*WB*, p. 133). Earlier in the novel, as a further sign of his complicity, the magistrate has had recourse to a teleological version of history when he claims that the historical record will exonerate him, and condemn Joll's barbarism (*WB*, p. 114). There is, however, an alternative history in the novel: it is the story of the magistrate's personal growth, simmering in his subconscious, and made manifest through a sequence of dreams. Unlike the other narrative forms alluded to, the dream sequence is non-linear (unlike a memoir or a confession), and non-circular (unlike literary pastoral). Its logic is, instead, accretive and progressive.

The first dream is of children building a snowcastle in the square of the settlement, with a perhaps older girl, clearly evoking the barbarian girl. As the sequence progresses, the barbarian girl is unequivocally identified, and the 'building' activity embraces a replica of the town and the act of baking bread. There is a movement away from sexual speculation and towards images of community and sustenance in the sequence. In each case, the magistrate is thwarted from intervening, or acting as he wishes; and this becomes important in the final scene, where there is an echo of the dream when the magistrate comes upon some children building a snowman in the square, and he resists the urge to interfere, observing that the snowman will need arms. The dream scenario is finally realized in the world of the novel, and the magistrate refrains from projecting his own scheme. There is something purposive in this that is clearly at odds with the mood of the final sentence, where he reports feeling 'like a man who has lost his way long ago but presses on along a road that may lead nowhere' (*WB*, p. 156). The dream sequence, finally irrupting into the world of the novel, presents a narrative of sublimation and advancement that may be *dependent* on the magistrate losing his way in the linear sense. In this connection, the road metaphor is pointed, but must be read in a way that opposes the magistrate's implied reading of it.

Life and Times of Michael K

The problem of how the individual should be situated in relation to history becomes the driving concern in *Life and Times of Michael K* (1983). The title calls up a narrative tradition, which embraces non-fictional modes such as the political memoir as well as the novel, in which individual engagement with social and historical events is the principal point of interest. Coetzee's novel then ironically undermines this association by portraying an anti-hero whose *raison d'être* is to resist all forms of social connection and political affiliation. This does not make the novel apolitical: its setting evokes the social breakdown and political unrest of South Africa in the 1980s very clearly. As with Coetzee's previous books, *Life and Times of Michael K* is constructed in such a way that it alludes to its context whilst avoiding a direct engagement with it.

Michael K is a simple South African – the reader infers he is non-white – subjected to the oppressions of apartheid (enforced labour, incarceration, and so on), while finding ways of eluding the mechanisms of state control. As the novel is set at a time of violent social breakdown, the instruments of control appear to have become intensified, and yet not fully effective, creating the space for a Michael K to live in the gaps. At the outset, K resigns from his position as a gardener working for the City of Cape Town, before being made redundant. He then sets out on a quest with his ailing mother to find the farm near Prince Albert where she had grown up. They need permits to travel by train, but as these do not arrive K constructs a barrow to transport his mother. She sickens on the journey, however, and dies in hospital at Stellenbosch. Bearing his mother's ashes, K eventually arrives at a deserted farm in the Prince Albert district, which may or may not be the one his mother described. He decides to bury her ashes here, and begins to cultivate some patches of land.

Michael K's experiences are punctuated with episodes of state interference or institutionalization. After his mother's death he is forced to work on a railway labour gang, briefly; and he is later picked up by the authorities and taken to the Jakkalsdrif camp in which the unemployed are interned to form a labour pool. He is then interned in the Kenilworth camp, and, in section 2 of the novel, narrated by the camp's medical officer, the issue of regulation and control receives its clearest exposition. The medical officer is driven to try and make K 'yield' his meaning, a metafictional idea that implicates both author and reader.

Before his first incarceration, K attempts to live his minimal existence on the deserted farm. His proprietorship is disturbed, however, by the arrival of the grandson of the family that owns the farm, the Visagies. The grandson, an army deserter, returning to a place of childhood security, embodies an ironic parallel with K. After escaping from Jakkalsdrif camp, K returns to the farm to cultivate a crop of pumpkins and melons. He is disturbed on this occasion by the arrival of a small revolutionary force from the mountains, though K is not detected. The idyll at the Prince Albert farm is eventually destroyed by the arrival of soldiers seeking the revolutionaries: they blow up the farmhouse, and take K to the Kenilworth camp. In the novel's brief final section, K returns to the Cape, having escaped once more. His perspective, incorporating a minimalist philosophy of survival, is conveyed in a lyrical closing passage.

Critics have been much exercised by the apparent reference to Kafka in the name Michael K, which inevitably brings to mind the protagonist of *The Trial*, Josef K. Teasingly, even while acknowledging the influence of Kafka on his work, Coetzee has said 'there is no monopoly on the letter K' (*DP*, p. 199), though it is clear that elements of Coetzee's treatment of marginalization and alienation are informed by Kafka. It is the preoccupation with elusiveness, however, that takes this kind of inspiration in new directions. The novel makes the problem of interpretation central, and gives the issue of elusiveness a material political edge, even though it retains its poststructuralist connotations. There is clearly an obvious parallel with Derridean notions of textuality in the elusiveness of Michael K; yet the way in which the novel is rooted in its context ensures that its treatments of textuality are more than mere abstractions. For example, the absence of any overt reference to Michael K's racial identity or appearance is a denial of apartheid's obsessive system of classification. He is equally resistant, however, to all social and political affiliation. Indeed, he embodies a principle of apolitical withdrawal, epitomized in his remark to the medical officer that he is 'not in the war' (*MK*, p. 138).

In one sense, then, the motif of textuality gives a purposive political edge to K's elusiveness; yet the issue is also ambiguous, because another feature of K's elusiveness is his propensity to fall silent, a sign of disenfranchisement as well as resistance. K's silence often colludes with his material oppression, as when he is rendered speechless by the arrival of the Visagie grandson at the farm at Prince Albert, and his efforts of cultivation are interrupted (*MK*, p. 60). This sense of disenfranchisement is finally offset, however, by the emergence of K's thoughts at the end of the novel, the section in which his philosophy of gardening is articulated. This establishes the moral high ground of the book, and a challenge to the oppressive text events.

The problem of interpreting and understanding Michael K is also a formal issue in the novel, obliging us to evaluate the third-person narrator's knowledge of the protagonist. Insofar as this narrator is a lingering convention from the realist novel, we are invited to wonder about the extent to which K's story is appropriated in the narrative mediation of sections 1 and 3. Such concerns are provoked especially by the second section, in which the medical officer makes his more overt attempts to interpret and appropriate K's story. If the first and third sections reveal a third-person narrator *speaking for* K – especially in the articulation of his thoughts – the second section trains us to worry about this tendency, which builds into the novel a self-conscious interrogation of its form, and its use of the realist code of omniscient narrative.

For Nadine Gordimer, in her important review of *Life and Times of Michael K*, there is a more damaging problem of political credibility in the novel, stemming directly from Coetzee's conception of a marginalized, disenfranchised protagonist, which, she feels, shows he 'does not recognize what the victims, seeing themselves as victims no longer, have done, are doing, and believe they must do for themselves.' Gordimer's review reveals a view about the function of the novel that is in direct opposition to Coetzee's conviction. She appeals to Georg Lukács' notion of typicality to explain the connection between public life and private destiny she finds wanting in Coetzee's novel. She also misses that unifying principle of narration that Lukács presents as an integral feature of realist writing, through which a coherent overview of the historical moment may emerge ('The Idea of Gardening', p. 6). Michael K is engaged with this debate about the function of the novel, but in such a way as to challenge Lukácsian principles, especially the conception of realism as an ordered narrative framework that makes sense of historical contradiction through an interpretive vantage point that is both necessary and blameless. In *Michael K*, Coetzee retains an element of this vantage point – an element of lingering realism – even while he questions its validity, transforming that dependency into a form of *revitalized* realism.

An indication of this revitalization is evident in the formal self-consciousness of the book, and in the contrasting narrative stances. The third-person narrator of sections 1 and 3 usually refrains from pronouncing judgement on K, a caution that contrasts with the desire of the medical officer to make K 'yield' his story (*MK*, p. 152). This jarring note has the effect of making the third-person narrator seem less controlling, less desirous of appropriating K's story, even though we might find traces of this impulse. This means that in the important final section there are fewer clear signs of third-person interference, and that K's thoughts, in the manner of a first-person monologue, are rendered in a form of free indirect discourse pushed to its limits (*MK*, pp. 182–4).

The formal arrangement of the book thus serves to prioritize the substance of K's closing thoughts. One element of these thoughts is K's philosophy of minimal subsistence, a principle that makes the kind of gardening he practises inherently political in that it stands in opposition to the regime of *farming* practised by the Visagies. K's temporary occupation of the farm thus has the air of political allegory about it. Given the running theme of pastoral in Coetzee's work, as a South African literary genre to be interrogated, there is clearly a revisionist element to this envisaging of a non-white establishing a temporary era of gardening on his own terms. This challenge to the Afrikaner rural idyll, the myth of a return to the land, lends the book a political significance – and ideological orientation – that it seems in other ways to avoid. Yet the idea of gardening has also a broader, ecological significance, linking the minimal existence that K embodies with the larger question of human subsistence.

The question of narrative voice is complicated, however, because the novel's language, as Derek Attridge has shown, is rich in literary allusion and cadence, so that the rendering of K's thoughts involves a method that 'constantly distances the narrative voice from the inner consciousness of the character' (*J. M. Coetzee and the Ethics of Reading*, p. 51). The effect of this is twofold: first, it reinforces our sense of K's otherness; and second, it makes the kind of interpretive efforts that the novel entices us to make problematic, simultaneously endorsed yet undermined by the novel's own operations.

In our pursuit of meaning, we may feel encouraged to read the story of Michael K as a story about the control of social space, and to note that this was another key facet of apartheid's systematic rule. When he eludes, or escapes internment, K is able to pursue his career as a cultivator. Incarceration is thus a counter-motif, set against gardening; and in the novel, incarceration carries the broader connotation of discipline exercised through institutions. In this respect, the novel reveals a Foucauldean preoccupation with the role of institutions in the socialization process. The Jakkalsdrif labour camp is an obvious instrument of social control, transforming the homeless into a workforce. The Kenilworth camp, originally a 'rehabilitation' camp, is re-designated as an 'internment' camp. As the civil war progresses, the policy hardens; but the important point is that 'labour battalions' can be supplied just as well from internment camps as rehabilitation camps. Disciplinary practices may change arbitrarily or unpredictably, Coetzee shows, in order to serve a particular end (*MK*, pp. 153–4).

Equally important is the association made between the camps and other forms of institution, such as schools and hospitals, which have a disciplinary function. The special school for 'afflicted and unfortunate children' attended by K, with its curriculum dominated by various forms of physical work, is another form of labour pool (*MK*, p. 4). (The parallel with the Jakkalsdrif camp is not lost on K (*MK*, p. 74).) Before arriving at Jakkalsdrif, K is taken to hospital while in police custody, a point that hints at another form of institutional control. K's mother dies in hospital in Stellenbosch, an event that K subsequently describes as the culmination of a life of disciplined labour (*MK*, p. 136).

In the important closing section, K's thoughts are given in a form of first-person monologue that summarizes his story and makes the camp motif central to it. He concludes:

> Perhaps the truth is that it is enough to be out of the camps, out of all the camps at the same time. Perhaps that is enough of an achievement, for the time being. How many people are there left who are neither locked up nor standing guard at the gate? I have escaped the camps.
>
> (*MK*, p. 182)

The extent of the book as a political allegory is obvious here, especially in relation to the practices of the apartheid regime. Yet the familiar complicating of the allegorical dimension is also apparent, especially as this passage also reveals aspects of an allegory of ideas. There is a claim to a kind of heroism in K's thoughts, where escaping the camps becomes an extraordinary achievement: the simple man is heroic in the challenge to disciplinary practices that he embodies. This makes him a target for those practices but also a kind of archetypal deviant. The elusiveness of K thus asserts a philosophy of Being that flies by the nets of socialization and institutional control. But it is impossible to detach this more abstract element of the book as allegory from its more immediate political context. Part of K's elusiveness, his defiance, is geo-political; and, in relation to apartheid South Africa, a regime founded on principles of 'zoning' and spatial control, his symbolic challenge inevitably connotes resistance to the particular brand of late-colonial oppression.

The way in which allegory is 'undone' in the novel is especially clear in the episodes involving the Visagie farm: on the face of it, K's time as a cultivator on the farm appears to form an allegory of repossession. There are a number of parallels, often ironic, that suggest this. For example, the farm, which K takes to be the farm of his mother's childhood, is also a focus of the Visagie grandson's nostalgia. Yet it is excess and indulgence (in the form of Christmas feasting) that informs the grandson's memories, the mirror image of K's simple and surreptitious gardening (*MK*, p. 61). When K returns to the farm from the Jakkalsdrif camp, and builds himself a burrow in which to live, shunning the abandoned farmhouse, he wonders if the grandson has also dug himself a hole in the veld, and is 'living a life parallel to his own' (*MK*, p. 103). K dismisses the idea as unlikely, but the point of such a parallel is to invite us to think through the apparent allegory of repossession in which K's reluctance to inhabit the farmhouse, and his rejection of the notion of founding 'a new house, a rival line', make him appear to stand for a new era, an era not of farming and accumulation, but of subsistence gardening (*MK*, pp. 98, 104). Through the parallel between K and the Visagie grandson, the novel reveals an allegory of repossession in which opposing views of the land suggest contrasting political phases.

K's elusiveness, however, serves to resist attempts to situate him in such a simple frame of meaning, with its ordered sets of oppositions: gardening/farming, subsistence/accumulation. When the soldiers blow up the farmhouse, destroy the pump and commandeer K's crop, the very site of the fanciful allegory of repossession is effaced. K retains his packet of seeds and his most important identity trait – potential cultivator – but without the site in which that potential might be realized. Part of the point here is to suggest that K's potential requires a different frame of meaning, independent of any associations with the Afrikaner farm: in this reading, the political allegory is worked through, and then dissolves.

That opposition, however, cannot be eradicated from the reader's mind, and remains part of the book's meaning; but the crucial part of this ambivalent treatment, which invites us to question the terms of the allegory, is that we also interrogate the external referents. We realize that the space does not exist in which K's identity as a potential cultivator could be fully realized, and this realization constitutes a bridge to the real that stems from the self-cancelling element of K's story. This is an enactment of that seminal deconstructive procedure in which a binary opposition is reversed and then undermined. The end result of such a procedure is to expose the hegemonic assumptions in a framework of interpretation. The gardening/farming, subsistence/accumulation parallel proceeds so that the oppositions are reversed, and then undermined. The mythic story of Michael K, and the allegory in *Michael K* the novel are both self-cancelling: the novel eludes final interpretation just as much as its central protagonist does. The final effect, however, is not to obscure meaning, but to lay it bare: the reader's interpretive assumptions are questioned as the function of allegory is critically examined, in a highly self-conscious novel that encourages comparable self-consciousness in its readers.

The novel ends with K's imagined return to the farm – not an event in the world of the novel – and the improvised use of a teaspoon to draw water from the damaged well (*MK*, pp. 183–4). This image of minimal existence surpasses all others in the novel, and installs a narrative loop, since the infant K, with his harelip, was fed with a teaspoon (*MK*, p. 3). If K endures, the narrative loop implies, he does so by virtue of his persistent, minimalist philosophy.

This philosophy places stress on K as a figure of Being, an idea that also unsettles the book's series of allusions to deconstruction. Insofar as deconstruction invalidates origins and privileges textuality, it challenges the idea of Being as a state of existence prior to knowledge. K now emerges as the embodiment of the principle of Being, in an apparent deconstruction of the novel's use of deconstruction. With this contradiction comes the temptation of a simpler idea of reference, with the presence of K symbolizing an oppressed people. It was the simple presence of the majority non-white population in South Africa that eventually made the geopolitical control engineered by the architects of apartheid impossible to sustain. There is this political anchor to the book as allegory; but it coexists, in an elusive novel, with the delineation of a form of unfettered textuality.

Foe

The subtle ambivalence of *Michael K* resists a mechanistic reading of the book as a product of a particular historical context even while that context is clearly evoked. This kind of duality has become a hallmark of Coetzee's fiction, particularly evident in the next novel *Foe* (1986) where a similar gestural bridge to the South African context is built. Once again Coetzee's preoccupation with textuality and the role of the novel is apparent; but there is also a poignant evocation of oppression, which is made to speak simultaneously to the business of literary history and to the problem of how the colonized other is silenced.

Foe is a highly 'literary' work, a postcolonial reworking of Daniel Defoe's *Robinson Crusoe*, containing important allusions to other works by Defoe. Its metafictional aspect, together with its literary self-consciousness, made it particularly amenable to contemporaneous academic ideas. Yet this is not a 'difficult' novel requiring specialized knowledge: the narrative remains appealing to a general readership. However, readers are invited to ponder the place of this novel in literary history, and it is Coetzee's choice of *Robinson Crusoe* as his basis that is important here. Not that this is an unusual choice – there have been many re-workings of *Robinson Crusoe* ('Robinsinades', as they are sometimes called) – but Coetzee gives a characteristically self-conscious and ambivalent twist to this dependency. In conventional accounts, Defoe is the father of the English novel, and *Robinson Crusoe* is a canonical English text. It has also been characterized as embodying the great myth of Western imperialism in the way it enthusiastically embraces the idea of 'civilizing' unknown territories and indigenous inhabitants, as a form of heroic endurance. It is this taint of colonialism that serves Coetzee's purpose particularly well, because he is able to observe a pointed historical correspondence: *Robinson Crusoe* was published in 1719, which is also the era of early Dutch settlement in South Africa, the Dutch East India Company having established a settlement at Cape Town in 1652.

This suggests an association between the origins of the English novel and the origins of colonialism in South Africa, both emanations of European imperialism – one cultural, the other political – with a common ideology of superiority. However, Coetzee is never as simplistic as this. Indeed, as a writer, he is admiring of Defoe's technical accomplishments and innovations, and has suggested that *Foe* is a tribute to eighteenth-century prose style (*DP*, p. 146). The literary allusiveness of the novel, in fact, heralds a complex treatment of the issue of canonicity, within which there is a writing back to Ian Watt, who established Defoe's formative role in the history of the novel in his classic work of criticism, *The Rise of the Novel*. The allusions to Defoe's work raise involved questions about power and textuality through (especially) a series of three prominent intertextual references, embedded within each other, in effect: these are *Robinson Crusoe*, *Roxana* (1724) and the short story or anecdote 'A True Revelation of the Apparition of One Mrs Veal' (1706).

It is the reworking of Crusoe that dominates the novel, of course. It is given a startlingly different emphasis by the introduction of Susan Barton as an intermediary to Cruso's story (Coetzee omits the 'e'). She seeks out Foe (as Defoe was originally called) in order to have the island story recorded. The pointed differences between her story and the published *Crusoe* reveal the imaginative premise: Coetzee invites us to speculate on the inspiration for *Crusoe*, and on the omissions and reconstructions evident in the finished novel – and, also, in the notional moment of the inception or 'fathering' of the novel genre.

Defoe's method, as every student of the novel knows, was to conceal artifice and appeal to verisimilitude. In its first edition, the title page of *Crusoe* makes no mention of the author and projects itself as an autobiographical account written by Crusoe himself. Coetzee, by contrast, is much concerned with literary artifice, and by reversing particular details from *Crusoe* he draws our attention to the implausibility of the original. Coetzee's Cruso feels no need for tools, for example, where the original Crusoe makes a number of trips to his wrecked ship to build a vast store of tools, guns, ammunition, canvas, food, razors, knives, and so on. (In Coetzee's novel it is Foe who is preoccupied with guns and tools.)

The differences also reveal Coetzee's Cruso to be a postcolonial figure. If Defoe's Crusoe is the archetypal colonialist, enamoured of the project of taming a new world, Cruso is emblematic of exhausted imperialism. Unlike his literary model, he makes no table or chair, no lamp or candle; he does not keep a journal, or build a boat. Neither does he have any seed to sow; but he does occupy himself with building barren terraces ready for planting.

There is a feminist dimension to *Foe*, as well as a postcolonial one, and these elements come together in the treatment of the two marginalized figures, Susan Barton and Friday, and the question of who controls the story that is told. Susan Barton is a version of the eponymous heroine of *Roxana*, whose first name is also Susan, and this second transtextual borrowing from Defoe complicates things considerably. We are invited to assume that Susan Barton's island story is the inspiration for *Crusoe*, but that the woman is written out and put in another of Defoe's novels instead (even though Foe suggests that the island story must be set within a longer narrative of Susan's experiences (*F*, p. 117)). Such a conceit invites us to think about the differences between the two novels, and to speculate on the patriarchal bent of their author: with the woman edited out, *Crusoe* is clearly a myth of masculine colonial endeavour and endurance, while Susan's challenge to the status quo is focused, in *Roxana*, on the economic and sexual basis of marriage – a challenge that is ultimately contained and condemned.

These invited speculations are one aspect merely of a rich and complex investigation of authorship and authority in *Foe*. In this connection Susan Barton emerges as an ambivalent figure. On the one hand, she is apparently at the mercy of Foe's invention – especially when she is dogged by the appearance of a daughter she does not believe is hers, in an echo of the daughter episode at the end of *Roxana*; on the other hand, however, she reveals affinities with Foe in their tussle for control of the island story. When she reflects that Cruso will be a disappointment to the world, that his tale will not satisfy the requirements of an adventure narrative, she anticipates Foe's determination to embellish the story (*F*, p. 34). The sense of Susan Barton's complicity is heavily qualified; but it is there, nevertheless, in the way in which her longings and desires are bound up with the need to assert control over her story.

When Barton expresses doubts about her identity at the end of the third section, in the form of the kind of ontological uncertainty that is common in postmodernist writing, she elicits from Foe some reflections on substantiality/insubstantiality, as well as his resonant account of how, 'in a life of writing books', he has often 'been lost in the maze of doubting' (*F*, p. 135). Foe's reflection on his 'blindness and incapacity' (*F*, p. 136) is also, of course, an articulation of the doubts and insecurities of the postcolonial writer, here projected back on the entire historical project of the novel in English.

As in most of Coetzee's novels, the problem of allegory, as a mode that is simultaneously evoked and interrogated, is central to *Foe*. The allegorical correspondences are clearest in connection with Friday, whose silence seems to suggest the repression of the black majority in South Africa. Susan Barton's wish to facilitate the telling of Friday's story, by teaching him to write, connotes the dilemma of the South African liberal. If we take the island to be an allegorical representation of modern South Africa, then Barton's summary of life there seems pointedly apolitical. Recognizing that 'all tyrannies and cruelties' were possible on the island, she celebrates the fact that 'we lived in peace with each other' as proof of an underlying human decency: 'our hearts had not betrayed us' (*F*, p. 37). In South Africa in the 1980s, the tyrannies and cruelties that might flow from civil war and social breakdown are averted by repressive state control as much as by a shared ethic of cooperation.

We are made to speculate about whether or not Friday has been castrated as well as having had his tongue cut out. As such details and speculations mount, he acquires a kind of mythic status that overloads any simple set of allegorical correspondences. The mutilated Friday is a figure of colonial oppression; but his scars begin to lend him an invulnerable authority, as the signs of historical oppression that constitute a story that is his own. And this speculation about Friday's story, which is at the heart of the novel, makes discourse the focus. Friday's silence is a form of resistance to the discourse that defines him; yet it is also a product of the world established in that dominant discourse. In a literary-historical sense, this lends the book an irreducible paradox. *Foe* depends upon *Robinson Crusoe* (and the tradition of novel writing that flows from it, in standard accounts); yet this defining Western literary myth is also exposed as bankrupt or exhausted by virtue of the gender and ethnic silences it reinforces. Yet 'speaking for' is no solution, and this is the apparent double bind that *Foe* insists upon: Friday must remain silent, his story untold, unless it is to be appropriated by the novelist tarnished with the brush of cultural imperialism. Coetzee here shows a greater sensitivity to the problem of appropriating the story of another than he had done in his previous novels.

Yet in the creation of Friday, Coetzee seeks to gesture beyond the double bind. In the scene where he draws upon the slate 'row upon row of eyes upon feet', these 'walking eyes' evoke images of slaves being forced to journey to places of enslavement; but they also suggest a sense of bearing witness, of a history of oppression that is not forgotten (*F*, p. 147). This sense of an alternative history waiting to be unleashed is the central idea of the novel's final section, where a new narrating persona – perhaps representing Coetzee – supplants Susan Barton. The crucial moment is when this new narrator 'dives' into the wreck to try and find a way of releasing Friday's story. Earlier, the problem of 'mak[ing] Friday speak, as well as the silence surrounding Friday' is configured as the answer to the question 'who will dive into the wreck?' Barton says: 'On the island I told Cruso it should be Friday . . . But if Friday cannot tell us what he sees, is Friday in my story any more than a figuring (or prefiguring) of another diver?' (*F*, p. 142). This condenses the problem of who is qualified to make known the revised history of the postcolonial world, and alerts us to the fact that the author/narrator of the novel's final section is not the ideal candidate: Friday would be the genuine submarine archaeologist for this process of revisionism.

The narrator of the final section has two attempts to make Friday speak, and it is the second such episode that carries the weightiest implications. In a bold metafictional gesture, the narrator comes upon the manuscript of Susan Barton's island experiences in Foe's chamber, and then slips 'overboard' into her text, and into the water above the shipwreck. He dives down to a wrecked ship, and finds the only signs of life coming from Friday. In the way that Coetzee attaches a paradoxically positive association to the scarred body in earlier works, especially *Waiting for the Barbarians*, we read here that 'this is a place where bodies are their own signs. It is the home of Friday'. The ship in which Friday is found seems to be a composite, having elements of the various ships in the novel, and it thus becomes a symbolic distillation of the separate vehicles of imperial adventure, and so appropriately Friday's 'home', the site where the mutilated and chained body reveals the scars of colonial history as the text of its own story. The 'voicing' of Friday's silence in the extraordinary gesture at the end of the novel implies this historical necessity. The release of this 'unending' history, which 'runs northward and southward to the ends of the earth', gestures towards a postcolonial future, but without actually articulating that history (*F*, p. 157).

Age of Iron

The extraordinary ending of *Foe* indicates a desire to cede authority to the oppressed other, and this gesture is one of a sequence of situations in Coetzee's works in which power and authority are relinquished. This is the central organizing idea of the next novel, *Age of Iron* (1990) in which the elderly Mrs Curren, a retired Classics lecturer, suffering from terminal bone cancer, undergoes a kind of personal dissolution which is also a form of qualified political enlightenment. Coetzee thus inverts the usual form of the novel of personal development to make Mrs Curren's 'progress' dependent upon her acceptance of her own unimportance as she approaches death.

On the day Mrs Curren's illness is diagnosed, she is 'adopted' by Vercueil, the alcoholic vagabond who becomes a kind of angel of death to her, though this allegorical idea, predictably, is held up for our critical scrutiny. The novel takes the form of a letter, written by Mrs Curren to her émigré daughter now based in North America. The unreliable Vercueil takes responsibility for posting the letter, which seems unlikely to the reader, making Mrs Curren's confessional narrative appear to be for herself only. To the extent that Vercueil is her confessor, as her companion, he fulfils this role only because he can give her no gift of redemption; and, in another inversion of convention, Coetzee implies that this is what makes Mrs Curren's confession genuine.

Her moral growth is accelerated by the deaths of two black boys, Bheki, her maid Florence's fifteen-year-old son, and his friend, both of whom are shot by police. Bheki's friend, who calls himself 'John', is killed at Mrs Curren's house, while hiding in Florence's quarters, a fact that accelerates her understanding of her complicity in the political structure.

Coetzee gives 1986–9 as the dates of composition (a period when South Africa was governed under a State of Emergency), and the scenes of township violence clearly evoke the unrest in Cape Town of 1986. The novel also registers a key contemporaneous principle of black opposition: that of non-white solidarity and non-cooperation. An increasingly militant youth, promoting a new wave of school boycotts, is a marked feature of this phase of black resistance, and this kind of attitude is reflected in Bheki's stance. Mrs Curren's liberal reflections on childhood are directly confronted and challenged by the comradeship of a new militant youth. There are, in fact, a number of uncharacteristically direct references to the political context in this novel. This sense of the novel's embeddedness in its immediate history makes it Coetzee's most engaged novel in the narrow historical and political sense, and the kind of intervention he has usually resisted. In a broader historical context, Mrs Curren understands that it is colonial history, and specifically Afrikaner Nationalism, that has produced this political interregnum of resistance, this 'age of iron', in which normal human relations are distorted.

This impulse towards direct representation sits alongside Coetzee's more usual literary self-consciousness in this novel, and this makes for a particularly powerful fusion. The customary debate about allegory is raised by the narrator herself (*AI*, p. 84), requiring us to consider the extent to which she stands for South Africa, the cancer within mirroring the diseased society without. The most dominant literary theme, however, is the novel's investigation of the confessional mode, for it is this aspect that conveys a sense of Mrs Curren's development towards relinquishing personal authority, despite the sense of her continuing intellectual intransigence in the face of social and political change that sometimes upsets her enshrined liberal values.

Coetzee's project in his treatment of confession can be understood with reference to his essay 'Confession and Double Thoughts: Tolstoy, Rousseau, Dostoevsky', in which a seemingly insurmountable problem is identified: the fact that the confessional mode of writing seems always to be derailed in its intentions by the fact of self-deception. Motives based on self-interest, or self-congratulation, produce a form of 'double thought', or 'the malaise that renders confession powerless to tell the truth and come to an end' (*DP*, p. 282). This means that the goal or end of confession – 'to tell the truth to and for oneself' – appears to be unattainable (*DP*, p. 291). For Coetzee, the notional authority of secular confession hinges on the confessant's ability to confront his worst failings (*DP*, p. 263). Yet double thought always seems to generate a hidden motive, thus compromising the 'truth' of a confession and preventing it from being brought to an end. A revealing example for

Coetzee is the death of Ippolit in Dostoevsky's *The Idiot*: Ippolit claims, because he is dying of tuberculosis, his confession must be seen as genuine since the moment before death creates a unique moment in which a genuine revelation of truth is possible (*DP*, p. 284). However, the prognosis of death is suspect, and his confessors do not accept Ippolit's sincerity, or his vow to kill himself, all of which destroys the possibility of establishing truth in the confession (*DP*, pp. 285–6). Coetzee's argument is that the revelation of truth cannot be forced, not even through the wilful act of advancing one's own death, since even this may be tainted by double thought (*DP*, p. 287).

Age of Iron seems to have been constructed in such a way as to confront the problem of double thought and the tainted confession. As Mrs Curren is dying essentially alone, any suspicion of self-interest may be absent in our reception of her narrative. She abandons her plan to turn her death into a public gesture through suicide, the kind of wilful act that might raise the suspicion of double thought. There is still the spectre of self-justification in the narrative, which notionally comprises a letter to her daughter to be delivered after her death. But there is a clear sense that the narrative functions primarily as a confession by and for the self – or, at least, that Coetzee is trying to construct a narrative situation that comes as close as possible to this confessional ideal, and to the revelation of truth.

A confession must be heard, of course, but the role of auditor is diluted and underplayed: the absent daughter fulfils this function, but only theoretically as the addressee; and Vercueil is often present as an auditor, but is unresponsive. The distanced reader also fulfils this function – indeed, 'hearing' the confession is part of the aesthetic experience of the novel. But there is no auditor or confessor to engage Mrs Curren in dialogue. Because of this, perhaps, she is able to progress towards the purity of a confession untainted by self-justification, but which follows the trajectory of self-knowledge. This is the essence of the answer she gives to her own query about why she is writing to her daughter, knowing that she must 'resist the craving' to share her death: 'To whom this writing then? The answer: to you but not to you; to me; to you in me' (*AI*, p. 5).

On her journey to some form of salvation, Mrs Curren's 'first confession' concerns her inability to love 'John', Bheki's unlikeable comrade; she senses that 'he is part of my salvation' (*AI*, pp. 124–5). The failure of her initial response is redressed after his shooting, and the way in which his final moments come to haunt her and to assume the status of a form of heroic final reckoning to parallel her own. This is another moment that speaks back to Coetzee's reflections on confession, and the difficulty of establishing authority in the moment before death. The balance of authority and death is reconfigured, here. Mrs Curren may be the confessant, susceptible to the imprisoning self-consciousness of double thought, but the authority that is established here comes by virtue of her sympathy for (and identification with) the authority in the moment before death associated with another. The 'hovering time' before the confrontation with 'the great white glare' is 'John's' moment of grace before facing the destructive force of the apartheid regime; but it is also Mrs Curren's goal, a timeless moment of self-reckoning in which the self is alone with the self in order, paradoxically, to transcend the drive of self-motivation (*AI*, p. 160).

Vercueil's unresponsiveness as a confessor is a seminal aspect of Coetzee's experiment with the confessional mode. When Mrs Curren makes her confession to him about the inadequacy of being good (when heroism is called for), she is coming to terms with the irrelevance of her erstwhile liberal ideas; but there is nothing to indicate that Vercueil has heard her, and her recounting of the episode (ostensibly to her daughter) reveals the point of this: 'is a true confession still true if it is not heard? Do you hear me, or have I put you to sleep too?' (*AI*, p. 151). Because the authority of the literary confession is undermined by the suspicions of the confessor, Coetzee may be implying that Mrs Curren's confession approaches truth precisely because it is *not* heard. The truth through self-knowledge that she gleans depends upon Vercueil's neutrality, which is also his incompetence as a confessor in the convention of this role. He is also deeply suspect as a reliable messenger, which makes the delivery of the letter, and the addressee's role as a distant auditor, improbable and also irrelevant to the reception of the novel.

Associated with this process of self-abnegation and renunciation is a development of Coetzee's ongoing investigation of the post-colonizer. The ontological doubt of the colonizer, graphically imagined in the first novel, *Dusklands*, here reaches a kind of conclusion. With reference to some family photographs, Mrs Curren reassesses the substantiality of her dynasty. In one, she describes the family photographed in a garden, a bed of melons to the left of the group, and she wonders 'was it my grandfather who got up at four in the icy morning' to water the crop:

> If not he, then whose was the garden rightfully? Who are the ghosts and who the presences? Who, outside the picture, leaning on their rakes, leaning on their spades, waiting to get back to work, lean also against the edge of the rectangle, bending it, bursting it in?
>
> (*AI*, p. 102)

This returns us to one of the questions posed through the writing of *Life and Times of Michael K*: the true gardeners, those who establish a morally sound principle of inhabitation, are the ghostly presences outside the picture, outside the set pieces of colonial history.

The disfigured hand of Vercueil also echoes earlier novels, recalling the scars or disfigurements associated with the marginalized figures in the other books – Michael K, Friday, the barbarian girl. When Mrs Curren holds Vercueil's disfigured hand in the face of police questioning (over harbouring 'John'), she aligns herself with the sign of suffering in the face of the oppressor, and reminds us of the positive connotation and authority Coetzee has frequently assigned to the disfigured, scarred or mutilated body in his novels, as the repository – and the 'text' – of colonial oppression.

Perhaps the most powerful echo of an earlier novel is found in Mrs Curren's maze metaphor to explain her situation. Where *Foe's* 'maze of doubting' was made to correspond with the precarious and paradoxical place occupied by Coetzee, Mrs Curren's ambivalent position is similarly summarized. She compares her letter – that is, the whole narrative – to a maze, and herself to a dog lost in the maze. Answering her own question as to why she does not call to God for help, she explains that he cannot reach her:

> God is another dog in another maze. I smell God and God smells me. I am the bitch in her time, God the male. God smells me, he can think of nothing else but finding me and taking me. Up and down the branches he bounds, scratching at the mesh. But he is lost as I am lost.
>
> (*AI*, p. 126)

This is a powerful re-conceptualization of agnosticism in the face of death, with 'passing over' refigured as animal procreative fulfilment, a blind urge in which God would participate were He not out of reach. Mrs Curren's maze metaphor raises the possibility of some form of absolution, but makes it simultaneously repugnant and unavailable: she remains trapped in her own secular maze. This, however, is an apt summary of Coetzee's confessional project here: a secular equivalent of absolution is central to Coetzee's ideas about the end of confession (*DP*, p. 252), and Mrs Curren's Godless maze, in which the (far from reassuring) presence of God is still felt, seems appropriate as a metaphor for Coetzee's narrative design in *Age of Iron*, which, through artifice, constructs the theoretical space in which an untainted confession can be heard. In this sense, Mrs Curren approaches 'the status of the confessant as a hero of the labyrinth' (*DP*, p. 263).

Age of Iron is Coetzee's last novel to be clearly written and set within the apartheid era, its evocation of 'heroism' finally conditioned by the historical juncture it confronts. As a summation of Coetzee's preoccupations to date, coupled with a new urgency, it achieves an intensity that is very much of the hovering time of political interregnum: the inevitability of the end of apartheid is a psychological given; yet there remain the last gasps, the last morbid symptoms of a vicious regime to be reckoned with.

Chapter 4

Works II

The Master of Petersburg

The Master of Petersburg (1994) marks a turning point in Coetzee's career. Published in the year of the first multiracial elections in South Africa, it is composed in the run-up to the final demise of apartheid, in the final phase of interregnum, following the release of Nelson Mandela from prison and the unbanning of the ANC in 1990. Written at this historical juncture of transition, it is in many ways Janus-faced. Its deliberations about revolutionary activities evoke many of the contemporaneous political concerns in a South Africa faced by the prospect of being ruled by a party headed (for obvious reasons) by revolutionary leaders rather than practised politicians. In this sense, the novel achieves some of the political relevance and urgency felt in *Age of Iron*. But the setting is nineteenth-century Russia, which signals a clear opening-out of the novel's concerns. It builds on earlier work in another way, by developing the theme of authorship and canonicity, previously expounded most comprehensively in *Foe*, and in such a way as to achieve a kind of punctuation point in Coetzee's oeuvre. The question of authorship is agonized over in later novels; but the complex metafictional treatment it receives here represents an extreme turning-inwards, and a kind of final statement. Ultimately, this seems to be Coetzee's darkest, and most difficult novel.

The problems about authorship and responsibility explored in *The Master of Petersburg* derive from problems in Dostoevsky's poetics, and the protagonist of the novel is Fyodor Dostoevsky himself. The book begins with the return of this fictionalized 'Dostoevsky' to St Petersburg in October 1869 (he has been staying in Dresden to avoid his creditors). The point of the journey is to collect the personal effects of his stepson Pavel, who has died in suspicious circumstances. Pavel's papers, however, include a terrorist hit list and are in the hands of the Tsarist police, with whom Dostoevsky becomes entangled in the kind of brush with authority that is familiar from the earlier novels. He moves in to Pavel's former lodgings, there commencing an affair with the landlady, and becoming fascinated with her daughter (who had been in love with Pavel).

Coetzee is not entirely faithful to his biographical sources (the real Dostoevsky was survived by his stepson, for instance), but he does rely on actual events and historical figures, most notably the nihilist and revolutionary Nechaev, who was linked with the murder of a fellow student called Ivanov, who had left Nechaev's group and may have been seen as a threat, as a potential informer. At the heart of the novel is the confrontation between Nechaev and Coetzee's 'Dostoevsky', and this confrontation links the novel's central ideas pertaining to questions of 'fathering', authorship, and morality.

As he did in *Foe*, Coetzee invites his readers to imagine a moment before the composition of an important European novel. The real Ivanov was killed in November 1869, and this was the event that sparked Dostoevsky's novel *The Devils*, or *The Possessed*, or *Demons* (as it is variously translated). In *The Master of Petersburg*, there are a number of correspondences, or partial correspondence with these sources – for example, there is a character called Ivanov who is murdered in November 1869, possibly by Nechaev. The burden of the allusions to Dostoevsky, however, is literary; and, while there are references to characters and ideas from several of his works, this element of the book is finally condensed into an engagement with a single chapter: this is the 'At Tikhon's' chapter, which was suppressed from *Demons*, and which now appears as an appendix in modern editions. Coetzee's focus then, in a refiguring of textual elusiveness, is an 'absent' text, retrieved from the margins of the European novel.

Dostoevsky's demons are those consuming ideas that drive his characters to desperate or evil acts, and especially when pursuing 'freedom' through militant revolutionary behaviour. The 'sin' that Dostoevsky traces in *Demons* is the rebellion against God that is implicit in the assertion of human autonomy; and this idea of autonomy is embodied most clearly in Stavrogin.

Coetzee adapts the idea of being 'possessed', and gives it a clearly secular inflexion; but he also draws on Dostoevsky's critique of ideological conditioning. The manipulative Nechaev, who tricks Coetzee's 'Dostoevsky' into making a statement about his stepson's death, is the ideologue for whom consuming ideas drive out all logic or reason, and who is displaced from any system of socialization or debate. Dostoevsky perceives him as 'a crystal winking in the light of the desert, self-enclosed, impregnable' (*MP*, pp. 201–2). The enticement of lucid ideas that are also reductive is aptly conveyed here. It is also worth noting that the image of the impregnable crystal is focalized by 'Dostoevsky' who thus retains the writer's vision – and moral authority – even though he feels he has lost his argument with Nechaev.

The focus of the debate between 'Dostoevsky' and Nechaev is the function of words, authorship, and the articulation of history. 'Dostoevsky' places emphasis on the responsibility taken on by the author of ideas, while Nechaev promotes a heady freedom in which there is no necessary connection between speech and thought to hinder the unpredictable acceleration of history: 'I can think one thing at one minute and another thing at another and it won't matter a pin as long as I *act*' (*MP*, p. 200). By extension, the effect of this is to deny the role of textuality in the construction of ideas; and this obliges us to revisit the problem of the rivalry between history and the novel which is continually present in Coetzee's work up to this point. The desire to act without reference to textuality, or the way in which ideas are constructed, is irrational, since ideas may become inconsequential or contradictory (though, presumably, still underpinned by some monolithic idea-demon, impervious to debate or revision). If Dostoevsky parodies the revolutionary position of the Nechaevites in *Demons*, Coetzee reorientates that parody to emphasize the writer's responsibility towards writing, and the complex and contradictory nature of the written word – an imperative demonstrated through the literary and theoretical allusiveness of *The Master of Petersburg*.

When Nechaev is seen effectively censoring the statement written by 'Dostoevsky', he repudiates the writer's desire for privacy, and, in effect, invokes the idea of state censorship. Thus, through Nechaev, Coetzee implies that the expectation of an unquestioning ideological conformity is the flipside of state control and censorship, and this speaks to Coetzee's position more generally. In the clash between Nechaev and 'Dostoevsky', Coetzee produces a powerful representation of the confrontation between writer and censor, which necessitates a self-confrontation for the writer who must identify his demons. Coetzee sees the way in which the oppressed individual is tainted by the activities of the oppressor to be paralleled in the clash between writer and censor.

Coetzee's appropriation of doubling, that familiar Dostoevskyan motif, is thus given a particular postcolonial inflexion, and one which speaks particularly to the position that Coetzee inhabits. The confessional mode is,

once again, the vehicle for a treatment raising questions of voice and contamination. The importance to Coetzee of *Demons* is that in this novel
Dostoevsky takes his 'last steps in the exploration of the limits of secular
confession' (*DP*, p. 287). In *Age of Iron*, Coetzee sought to exceed these limits
through an artful narrative construct. In *The Master of Petersburg* his strategy
for confronting these limits is an intertextual engagement with *Demons*, and,
more particularly, with the suppressed 'At Tikhon's' chapter, in which
Stavrogin gives the monk Tikhon his written confession. Stavrogin's crimes
include the apparent seduction of his landlady's fourteen-year-old daughter,
and his failure to intervene when he suspects the despairing girl is about to
commit suicide. In 'Confession and Double Thoughts: Tolstoy, Rousseau,
Dostoevsky', Coetzee points out that there is a mutual interrogation in 'At
Tikhon's': Tikhon is probing Stavrogin's motivation whilst Stavrogin is
evaluating Tikhon's credentials as confessor. The internal dialogue of first-
person confession is here exteriorised, with Tikhon pointing out the
anticipation of the receiver in Stavrogin's confession, and the compromised
motives this suggests.

Coetzee's analysis of *Demons* follows Bakhtin's in *Problems of Dostoevsky's
Poetics*, where Bakhtin observes that Tikhon's function is to open up the
circular monologism of Stavrogin's confession. The role of the right kind of
listener, following Bakhtin, can be conceived as productive, a way of
encouraging the other to grow and to change. The role of such characters in
unleashing the dialogic potential of the novel is significant, ameliorating the
problem of authorial control and the imposition of a monologic meaning.
The question of authority in *The Master of Petersburg* is examined through the
way Coetzee makes his novel, in one sense, an extended treatment of 'At
Tikhon's'. Stavrogin's crime against Matryosha, his landlady's daughter, is
projected onto 'Dostoevsky' when he takes rooms in Petersburg, and becomes
fascinated with the landlady's daughter (also named Matryosha). The author-
figure is therefore implicated in the crime that the real Dostoevsky will project
onto Stavrogin when he composes *Demons*. In the final chapter, 'Dostoevsky'
writes in Pavel's empty diary variations of scenes described in Stavrogin's
confession, a form of betrayal of the stepson that casts a shadow over the
authorial role, and which compounds the mistrust of 'Dostoevsky' fostered by
his predatory sexuality.

If the allusions to 'At Tikhon's' serve to make us question authorial power,
or 'the dance of the pen' (*MP*, p. 236), there is also, however, a potentially
redemptive motive, since this power may be seen as an allusion to the
taint of the colonizer or the ideologue compromising the writer's identity.
And since the recognition of that shadow also opens up the possibility of

self-confrontation, through dialogue with the pernicious voice of the censor or oppressor, there is the glimmer of the possibility of dialogic progress. Insofar as *The Master of Petersburg* insists on the compromised, the divided authorial self, it is an extended form of excoriatingly honest confession in itself. The disturbing sense of truth that emerges is then the foundation for future ethical progress.

There is also the sense that 'betrayal' becomes a figure for authorial self-relinquishment, and so a potential route through which authority or rigid control gives way to something more propitious or exploratory. In the final chapter 'Dostoevsky' imagines a future Pavel and projects onto him the kind of doubleness that will inform *Demons*, regardless of any claims of sentiment or personal duty. Yet, as we have seen, doubleness can be both taint and the basis for advancement; and an apt way of accounting for the ambivalent demon that possesses the post-colonizer, the union of self and other, and a split literary and historical identity.

Coetzee's work up to and including *The Master of Petersburg* acknowledges the power of contemporary politics to restrict the imagination of the writer, even while each novel to this point participates in his ongoing struggle to resist the dominance of the political over the literary. An inevitable aspect of that 'rivalry' with history, however, is to highlight the anxiety of creative confinement, and the association readers may make between writer, work, and the late-colonial situation of apartheid South Africa (as I have been doing in this book). As apartheid recedes into history, however, such a chain of association becomes less compelling. The particular kind of intensity that drove his work up until this point, and which manifested itself in ever more tortured expressions of complicity, has given way to different kinds of fictional exploration.

One issue that remains particularly fraught in Coetzee's work – but one which has become increasingly open to a variety of treatments, is the representation of violence. This issue has always been taxing for Coetzee, given that his career has seen him repeatedly push the limits of inventiveness to prevent politics overwhelming the literary. The risks he has run include (*In the Heart of the Country*) the depiction of the rape of a white woman by a black man in the exploration of postcolonial intellectual repression, risky for the white liberal writer because the fantasy about the black rapist is a recurring topos in the discourse of racism. In that novel, however, its unsettling postmodernist credentials made the certainty of event open to doubt, and secondary to the investigation of how discourse constructs the self: as Magda puts it, 'I make it all up in order that it shall make me up' (*IHC*, p. 73).

Disgrace

In *Disgrace* (1999), Coetzee's next novel after *The Master of Petersburg* and an explicit engagement with post-apartheid South Africa, the multiple rape of a white woman by black men is a focal point. And because this novel is more bluntly realistic than Coetzee's earlier novels, the ameliorating effect that conditions the reception of the rape in *In the Heart of the Country* is not present. The event itself is not described, but it is felt to be a brutal retributive act, with the victim, David Lurie's daughter Lucy, seeming to accept with some fatalism that 'it was history speaking' through the rapists' (*Dis*, p. 156). Lucy takes no legal action against her attackers, and accepts the dubious arrangement offered by her neighbour Petrus – that is, to become an additional 'wife' to him, in exchange for his protection (*Dis*, p. 200). In doing so, she becomes the victim of blackmail and extortion. It is impossible for the reader not to draw a parallel between the sexually predatory Lurie and his daughter's rapists; and this suggests a depressing lesson in the legacy of colonialism, as power shifts and Petrus's expansionist designs on Lucy's land mirror the careless acquisitive habits of the colonizer.

There is, however, an important development of the theme of absolution – or the secular equivalent of absolution – that is so prominent in both *Age of Iron* and *The Master of Petersburg*. In those novels, however, Coetzee had been experimenting with the confessional mode, whereas here he approaches the problem rather differently. Confession then becomes a tool for the regulated society to imprison individual consciousness, and is thus emptied of its true purpose. When Lurie is brought before the committee convened to consider the complaint brought by Melanie Isaacs, the student with whom he has had an affair, he is forced to make a 'confession' of guilt (*Dis*, pp. 51–2) by members of the committee who have plainly prejudged the issue. Coetzee here stoops to producing, in Dr Farodia Rassool, a caricature of the unswerving feminist who wants only a confession to the 'abuse of a young woman', and not Lurie's fanciful confession that he 'became a servant of Eros' (*Dis*, p. 53). Where Colonel Joll's pursuit of truth/pain in *Waiting for the Barbarians* opened into an allegorical dimension, addressing the imperial mindset as well as the mutability of language, the exposure of 'interrogation' in *Disgrace* seems more a familiar denunciation of political correctness.

Coetzee shows how easily the tramlines of liberal thinking produce unintended regulatory effects; and the purpose of this is to demonstrate that sensitivity to the other is not an automatic capacity for the liberal sensibility, which may be alienated by a 'confession' that does not fit certain normative codes. Critics of South Africa's Truth and Reconciliation Commission (TRC) felt that its approach to the 'truth' was sometimes highly selective; and Coetzee's depiction of a quasi-legal hearing, where justice is predetermined, clearly evokes the contemporaneous concerns about the operations of the TRC, as we saw in chapter 2.

If the immediate (and depressing) political dimension to *Disgrace* is more immediate than in previous Coetzee novels, one might wonder if that felt imperative to rival history has become less pressing for him. An explanation for the difference seems to be that Coetzee here eschews the complex and ambivalent use of allegory that structures much of his earlier work. This avoidance signals a shift of emphasis, and there is certainly a distinct change of mood when one compares the early Cape Town chapters with the scenes centred on Lucy's smallholding, and, especially, the strange journey of partial moral growth that Lurie is engaged upon; and ultimately, the second half of the book reveals a fresh consideration of the issue of resistance.

Any reader of Coetzee soon becomes familiar with the significance of resistance in his work – whether this suggests the individual's resistance of pre-given social patterns, or the resistance of the novels and the characters within them, when an attempt is made to interpret them, or reduce them to recognizable patterns of meaning. Part of the pleasure of reading Coetzee is then the part played by particular textual features that put readers through a complex and indeterminate reading experience, involving (for example) the simultaneous anticipation and distrust of allegory. In this way, Coetzee encourages his readers to supply a template of meaning which must then be re-evaluated because of its evident incompleteness or because of the complicity it has seemed to encourage.

One of the effects of this process is to encourage doubts about interpretation generally, with professional criticism at the sharp end of the judgement. We begin to wonder if Coetzee's own judgement of criticism is unavoidable: 'what can it ever be, but either a betrayal (the usual case) or an overpowering (the rarer case) of its object? How often is there an equal marriage?' (*DP*, p. 61). For much of his career – and especially in the novels written during the apartheid era – this preoccupation has had a clear postcolonial significance. Coetzee's readers find themselves keeping in check the impulse to simplify or explain, where a text provokingly eludes their grasp. And this process puts readers in the situation of the archetypal colonizer, armed with pre-given codes for understanding the world, and bringing discovered territories or peoples to order.

The function of the character Michael K, for example, is, as we saw in chapter 3, expressly related to the problem of textual meaning, which is problematized especially through the desire to make K 'yield' his story (*MK*, p. 152). The reader is made to share this desire with the medical officer who, in an important moment in the novel, imagines pursuing K, calling out to him his interpretation that K's stay in the camp was an allegory of 'how outrageously a meaning can take up residence in a system without becoming a term in it' (*MK*, p. 166). This is a rich and complex moment, and thoroughly representative of Coetzee's art in the first part of his career. The richness comes from the familiar ambivalence about allegory, in which different ideas or levels of allegory are simultaneously in play: there is the political allegory that structures the book, but which K attempts to resist; there is the poststructuralist allegory of the deferral of meaning, which is also thrown into doubt by the materiality of K, and the preoccupation with matters of subsistence. Most simply, perhaps, the novel stages an allegory of our reading of it, and it is this that elicits from us a dual response to the medical officer, with whom we share a sense of urgency to interpret K, and the dawning recognition that he is somehow beyond the 'system' that still contains him.

The purpose of this brief recap is to demonstrate the new direction represented by *Disgrace*, where ideas of allegory are not raised so explicitly, and are, in effect, subjected to still greater critical scrutiny. To demonstrate the point I shall consider a celebrated passage from *Disgrace*, in which an allegory of reading and interpretation seems to coexist with a literal representation. In the episode in question, we learn why Lurie decides to take responsibility for the dogs' corpses, after they have been humanely killed at the Animal Welfare League clinic. Witnessing the hospital workmen overseeing the process of incineration, he is dismayed to see how they confront the problem of the stiffened corpses, where the animals' dead legs catch in the trolley that sends them into the furnace, so that 'when the trolley came back from its trip to the furnace, the dog would as often as not come riding back too, blackened and grinning, smelling of singed fur, its plastic covering burnt away'. Lurie observes how 'the workmen began to beat the bags with the backs of their shovels before loading them, to break the rigid limbs'; and it is this that makes him take the job over:

> Why has he taken on this job? To lighten the burden on Bev Shaw? For that it would be enough to drop off the bags at the dump and drive away. For the sake of the dogs? But the dogs are dead; and what do dogs know of honour and dishonour anyway?
>
> For himself, then. For his idea of the world, a world in which men do not use shovels to beat corpses into a more convenient shape for processing.

The dogs are brought to the clinic because they are unwanted: *because we are too menny*. That is where he enters their lives.

(*Dis*, pp. 145–6)

The seasoned reader of Coetzee, accustomed to finding deliberations on power and textual meaning in the novels, might be inclined to read the use of 'shovels to beat corpses into a more convenient shape for processing' as a metaphor for the critical betrayal or mastery of a text, 'processed' by the critic careless of the text's aesthetic unity. Coetzee, after all, surely stands for a world in which critics do not do 'violence' to works of literature, in the same way that Lurie comes to stand for a world in which men do not beat corpses for disposal. The parallel is bound to be observed, yet the reader is equally bound to feel uncomfortable for observing it. As Coetzee knows, the depiction of a dead dog in literature can always be taken as a metaphor for something else; but the particular context of *Disgrace*, in which an empathic response to the plight of unwanted dogs is absolutely required, makes the pursuit of metaphor seem both unresponsive and reductive. We may even consider such a reading to be an unethical appropriation, in the final analysis, however much the text entraps us by eliciting this response.

Part of Coetzee's point, here, is to lead us away from a purely rational reading. After all, in a purely rational reaction we might baulk entirely at Lurie's idea that a corpse – and especially the corpse of an animal – can be 'dishonoured'. This opens up the realm of the literary in a compelling way, enabling Coetzee to move his readers to empathize with Lurie's position, regardless of the fact that such readers might be immune to the persuasion of rational argument on this matter. In a typically self-conscious way, Coetzee is examining the literary uses of pathos and sentimentality, qualities that reveal an enduring potential even though they are often considered in pejorative terms. In the passage quoted above, the reference to Little Father Time and the children's suicide in *Jude the Obscure* –'done because we are too menny' – puts Coetzee's purpose in a clear literary-historical perspective, since he is alluding to what is probably the most troublingly sentimental moment in Hardy's novels. Yet the implicit claim is for the clarity that emerges from pathos. (In the case of this episode in *Jude the Obscure*, the key social issues of education and inequality are imprinted on the reader's consciousness *because* of the overblown tragic episode.)

This is not to suggest that Coetzee's previous novels have been free from affecting moments of sentiment; but there is a shifting balance to be observed in Coetzee's work since *The Master of Petersburg* that lends greater prominence to questions of affect, and which facilitates the foregrounding of particular issues. In these later works, Coetzee has sometimes seemed to be searching for a spareness in his writing, a new form of 'truth', perhaps, as in the unflinching honesty of *Youth*. In that 'autobiographical fiction' Coetzee insists on rendering baser motives (which, the reader will speculate, may have been his own), without amelioration. The parallel pursuit in the fiction for a 'purer' form of expression – even though this may be revealed as impossible – facilitates a less ambiguous engagement with philosophical issues.

Although the novels written during the apartheid era were written to promote a special kind of resistance to the pressures of politics, it does now seem that that pressure issued in an intensity – and complexity of meaning – that has become less apparent in Coetzee's work in the post-apartheid era. As the ideological squeeze on literature has been felt less, Coetzee has been freed up to treat literary and ethical concerns, without viewing these through the prism of colonial violence, with the particular inflection of personal complicity that issue had lent to the earlier novels.

The Lives of Animals and *Elizabeth Costello*

There is, then, a clear difference between 'The Narrative of Jacobus Coetzee', in Coetzee's first book *Dusklands*, which re-imagines the horrors of that form of colonial violence perpetrated by eighteenth-century explorers of the Cape, and a novel from Coetzee's later creative phase such as *Elizabeth Costello* (2003). These two novels are also linked, however, by the problem of depicting violence in fiction; but in the later novel the kind of philosophical exploration that begins to emerge in *Disgrace* is developed further.

Elizabeth Costello can be grouped together with *Disgrace* and *The Lives of Animals* (1999), which is subsumed in *Elizabeth Costello*. This is a phase of writing in which Coetzee concerned himself with questions arising from debates about animal rights. The precise focus is the problem of how the aesthetic effects and ethical questions generated by literature bear on the relationship between human beings and the rest of nature.

The Lives of Animals is worth considering separately from *Elizabeth Costello*, because its emphases are obscured in the longer work, where the inconsistency of Costello becomes more obvious. In *The Lives of Animals* there is a much clearer invitation to evaluate Costello's intellectual position, and to imagine sharing her 'literal cast of mind' (if we do not already) – for example when she insists that 'when Kafka writes about an ape', he is 'talking in the first place about an ape' (*LA*, p. 32). This puts Coetzee's constant preoccupation with how literature is distanced from reality in the same configuration found in the description of the dead dogs in *Disgrace*. Again, we wonder if the consideration of animals should not be read in a metaphorical manner. There is an implicit suggestion that the problem of animal rights, as an irreducibly material ethical issue, puts the question of literary aesthetics into a fresh perspective; and that if this implies a challenge to given cultural and epistemological boundaries – the utilitarian evaluation of animals (a legacy of Enlightenment rationality) – such a challenge may also have a bearing on the teaching and reception of literature.

There is also a suspicion – and, perhaps, an invitation to explore the suspicion – that Costello might be the author's mouthpiece (although this is ultimately irresolvable). In this connection, it is interesting to note, for example, that in an earlier essay Coetzee rehearses an argument against the 'species argument' that permits the killing and consumption of some animals, but not others, and wonders 'is it fair to remind ourselves of the Nazis, who divided humankind into two species, those whose deaths mattered more and those whose deaths mattered less?' ('Meat Country', p. 45). Costello's views are challenged by other characters in the narrative – sometimes forcefully – though she is invariably in the moral ascendancy, even when she is on intellectually shaky ground.

Costello (and so Coetzee) is well versed in moral philosophy and animal rights. Her challenge to 'speciesism', the privileging of the human species, may have intellectual credentials; but what lends the work a fictional element, anticipating the novel, is the way in which Coetzee takes his readers beyond a straightforward engagement with the arguments, encouraging us to allow sympathy to weigh more heavily in the balance. In the domestic drama, for example, the hostility of Costello's daughter-in-law Norma tends to undermine her intellectual position. This is important because Norma makes the crucial observation that 'there is no position outside of reason where you can stand and lecture about reason and pass judgment on reason' (*LA*, p. 48). Because we are learning to sympathize with Costello rather than Norma, this difficulty – which could sink Costello's position entirely – carries less weight than it might. As with the disposal of the dead dogs in *Disgrace*, Coetzee's readers experience the principle by which sympathy is privileged over reason.

The objection to reason is also part of Costello's intellectual position – the paradox observed by Norma – and this objection is articulated most clearly in the account of experiments on an ape in a cage, experiments designed to test his problem-solving skills when his food is placed increasingly further from reach. Costello suggests that the thoughts of an ape in such an experiment might conceivably be focused on its relationship to its captors –'why is he starving me? . . . Why has he stopped liking me?' – rather than the practical, problem-solving question that is assumed: 'how does one use the stick to reach the bananas?' (*LA*, pp. 28–9). In this speculation, the ape is led away from 'the purity of speculation' and towards 'lower, practical, instrumental reason'. This opposition assumes a central importance for Costello, who opposes 'practical reason' with 'ethics and metaphysics', and privileges 'fullness, embodiedness' over 'thinking, cogitation' (*LA*, p. 33). Insisting that 'there are no bounds to the sympathetic imagination', she lauds the faculty of the heart 'that allows us to share at times the being of another' (*LA*, pp. 34–5). Self-consciously, Coetzee makes what we might call an ecocritical claim for literature in this connection when, in the seminar presentation in 'The Poets and the Animals', Costello seeks to demonstrate the boundlessness of the sympathetic imagination in her reading of Ted Hughes's poems 'The Jaguar' and 'Second Glance at a Jaguar' (*LA*, pp. 50–55).

The effect of *The Lives of Animals*, and of *Elizabeth Costello*, is to promote the sympathetic capacity while simultaneously exposing its intellectual flaws. We must conclude that the sympathetic faculty, which the literary effect can promote, is fostered through intellectual effort, just as Costello's war with reason has to be conducted through a process of careful reasoning. Costello's experiences demonstrate that it is the essence of our being to be caught between sympathy and reason, much as Coetzee's text puts his readers through the same contradictory experience. The wisdom of Costello – and of Coetzee – is to seek to embrace this contradiction.

Ultimately *The Lives of Animals* becomes less of an intervention in the debate about animal rights and more a practical demonstration of human experience rooted in paradox and contradiction. This is especially telling where an ecological worldview is called into question, as when Costello is struck by the irony that the knowledge and appreciation of ecosystems can be comprehended by human beings alone, and so cannot lead to a state of at-oneness. She realizes that the capacity for sympathy, for a different kind of being-in-the-world, is simultaneously facilitated, yet frustrated by humanity's intellect (*LA*, pp. 53–4).

In *Elizabeth Costello* the attempt to embrace paradox is enhanced by the much clearer critique of Costello that emerges. Yet even this is complicated by the fictional frame. Costello's own experience of violence, when she was savagely beaten by a man at the age of nineteen (*EC*, pp. 165–6), appears to give her some authority on the topic of 'evil'. However, the reflection that this is a male author imagining female suffering is a complicating factor. This demonstration of sympathetic imagination on the author's part may have been motivated by a response to that restrictive form of rational reading in which some instances of authorial self-projection are deemed unacceptable.

The paradox that dominates *The Lives of Animals* – that reason is required to establish the limits of reason and the nurturing of sympathy – is developed in *Elizabeth Costello* in such a way as to take us to the heart of Costello's (and perhaps Coetzee's) predicament. Here the wistful hankering after spareness and immediacy of expression is conveyed in a directly confessional moment, in which such poignant directness is also shown to be immediately susceptible to appropriation, reinterpretation. In an extraordinary scene at the end of the novel Costello is depicted petitioning 'at the gate' of Heaven. To pass, she is required to account for her beliefs, as embodied in the conduct of her life, before a board of judges. At her first hearing she claims not to have any beliefs, and so fails; but she is given a second hearing where she makes a different sort of petition. She conjures a statement of belief of sorts from a childhood memory of rural Victoria, on the river Dulgannon. She recalls how 'tens of thousands of little frogs' would be woken from their 'tombs' in the sun-baked mud following seasonal 'torrential rains'. Costello is apologetic for her lyrical impulse in recounting the memory, but explains, whereas in her role as 'a professional writer' she conceals 'the extravagances of the imagination', she has decided, 'for this occasion', to 'conceal nothing, bare all' in a story presented 'transparently, without disguise'.

Her reason for striving for this immediacy is to get to the essence of her belief: 'In my account, for whose many failings I beg your pardon, the life cycle of the frog may sound allegorical, but to the frogs themselves it is no allegory, it is the thing itself, the only thing.' It is this attempt at laying things bare that enables her to articulate her belief: 'What do I believe? I believe in those little frogs . . . It is because of the indifference of those little frogs to my belief . . . that I believe in them' (*EC*, pp. 216–17).

Costello, here, offers a paean to nature, without the ordering self-consciousness of the professional writer; though we are still conscious of the conceit that this is the novelist's eye, producing something of elemental value as a way of justifying her existence. There is, however, a notional distinction between Coetzee and Costello here: whereas he is inventing a fictional moment of some originality and intensity to generate his effects, she is apparently finished with fiction, since she doubts its benefits (*EC*, p. 160), and its goodness (*EC*, p. 167). Without rhetorical guile, her petition is rooted in the power of a witnessed natural event, the allegorical dimension to which she tries to suppress. Yet it is the allegorical dimension that resonates with her judges (*EC*, pp. 218, 220) and, probably, with readers of the novel, though readers accustomed to Coetzee's ambivalent treatments of allegory will not miss the author's irony here. There is also a simple association of kinds of signification in the affinity between Coetzee and Costello, or, more simply, a parallel between Costello's belief in the frogs, and Coetzee's enduring belief in fiction. And this underscores Coetzee's irony: the writer cannot escape the imposition of metaphorical levels on his or her expression, and this may produce a nightmarish sense of being misunderstood, summarized in the parodically Kafkaesque experience 'at the gate' that ends the novel. It is a powerful moment in which Coetzee expresses something about the limits of fiction and of the writer's authority, and yet also demonstrates the enduring power or value of fiction.

Elizabeth Costello had a complex publishing history, since Coetzee delivered many of the sections as lectures over a period of years, and much of the book was published piecemeal between 1997 and 2003 (often in versions that are adapted for the novel), either in journals or in the form of pamphlets. The genre of the 'story-as-lecture', which produced *The Lives of Animals* and then gestated into *Elizabeth Costello*, figures also in Coetzee's Nobel Lecture of 2003, 'He and His Man', in which related questions about the nature of fiction are raised. ('He and His Man' draws on two more works by Daniel Defoe, *Tour through the Whole Island of Great Britain* and *Journal of the Plague Year*.) Returning to his preoccupation with Defoe and Crusoe, Coetzee here produces a fresh conceit: the 'He' is Crusoe, and 'His Man' is the fictionalised Defoe that 'He', Crusoe, is inventing.

Slow Man

Coetzee's preoccupation with investigating the bounds of fiction has taken an increasingly self-conscious and metafictional turn in his most recent fiction. In *Slow Man* (2005) Elizabeth Costello reappears as a character, but also, apparently, as the author of the fiction. The novel begins with an arresting but simple narrative situation: Paul Rayment, an Australian progressing quietly towards old age, is hit by a car whilst cycling, and is thrown through the air. He survives, but his injuries result in his having a leg amputated above the knee. His life is thrown into further turmoil when he falls in love with the nurse he employs to care for him – a married Croatian woman called Marijana Jokić. The plot generates a number of interesting global themes, which are also pressing in Australian society: the treatment of economic migrancy and the related question of national belonging is particularly noteworthy. However, the novel threatens to break its frame disastrously when, a third of the way in, Elizabeth Costello turns up at Rayment's door. She recites the opening words of the novel for him (concerning his accident), and explains: 'you came to me . . . in certain respects I am not in command of what comes to me' (*SM*, p. 81). The antagonism between Rayment and Costello, established in this scene, and which governs the mood of much of the novel, sets in train an extended disquisition on the nature of fiction – but also on the issue of authorial inspiration – that, for some readers, turns the novel into something of an exercise.

The portrayal of the Jokić family raises the great twenty-first century theme of migrancy, and especially the status of refugees. Costello has conceived the husband, Miroslav, as a 'Croatian refugee' (*SM*, p. 81); but it is through the son, Drago, that Coetzee makes the theme of identity and belonging particularly noteworthy. Rayment is himself rootless, having had 'three doses of the immigrant experience': he was brought to Australia as a child from his native France, asserted his 'independence and returned to France', but 'gave up on France and came back to Australia' (*SM*, p. 192). When he seeks to attach himself to the Jokić family he formulates the idea of sponsoring Drago's education, in a form of sublimation of his love for the mother.

The theme of social integration and national history is given particular poignancy through the business of Rayment's photograph collection. He is a retired photographer (who had specialized in portraits), and has amassed a collection of photographic portraits of early immigrant life in Australia, specifically 'photographs and postcards of life in the early mining camps of Victoria and New South Wales'. His collection includes some pictures taken by the noted nineteenth-century photographer Antoine Fauchery (1823–61). He plans to bequeath his collection to the State Library in Adelaide, in a gesture that will involve him in the national life (*SM*, pp. 48–9).

Explaining this intention to Drago later in the novel, he finds himself moved as they contemplate one of his Faucherys, and he speaks of 'our historical record'. We are made privy to Rayment's reflections as he tries to explain to himself why he is close to tears, and understands that it has to do with the putative shared national history that is implied:

> Just possibly this image before them, this distribution of particles of silver that records the way the sunlight fell, one day in 1855, on the faces of two long-dead Irishwomen, an image in whose making he, the little boy from Lourdes, had no part and in which Drago, son of Dubrovnik, has had no part either, may, like a mystical charm – *I was here, I lived, I suffered* – have the power to draw them together.
>
> (*SM*, p. 177)

When Drago subsequently doctors one of Rayment's Faucherys, apparently as a joke, the idealistic and reverent notion of a shared history of migrancy is put in a fresh perspective. Using digital technology, Drago has produced a sepia-coloured print with a superimposed image of his father, dressed to blend in with 'those stern-faced Cornish and Irish miners of a bygone age' (*SM*, p. 218). It is Costello who draws the forgery to Rayment's attention, thus signalling that the issue of authenticity is one of Coetzee's chief metafictional concerns in this novel (which may be obvious enough), and that, more importantly, the locus of this preoccupation is the new moment of global identity.

At the point where he explains his immigrant experience, Rayment also explains that his name rhymes 'with *vraiment*', thus establishing a notional equation between his idea of authenticity and the pursuit of a national history inflected with the successive waves of change that migrancy brings. Drago's forgery unsettles this neat equation, and represents a lesson of sorts for Rayment. There follows a scene of confrontation in which Rayment and Costello visit Marijana and Rayment requests the return of the original Fauchery now missing from his collection. Marijana protests that a photograph is not an 'original'; she shows her visitors Drago's room, with two doctored Faucherys on the wall, 'blown up to poster size'. In her broken English, she contests the idea of ownership implicit in Rayment's preoccupation with the original Fauchery: 'images is free – your image, my image. Is not secret what Drago is doing. These photographs . . . all on his website. Anyone can see' (*SM*, p. 249).

The point at issue, we come to realize, is not whether or not Marijana displays 'sophistry', or if Rayment is justified in doggedly trying to track down his 'original print' (*SM*, p. 245). Rayment has to relinquish his egotistical desire to be identified as the author of this particular contribution to Australian history, a desire that pulls against the collective ideal that is, ostensibly, his objective. Yet, hovering over the exchange between Rayment and Marijana is the notion that the world of the simulacrum, facilitated exponentially by the digital age and developing global communications, threatens the perception of identity on a human scale. It is not just a traditional notion of national identity that is impossible to sustain, but any stable record of historical change. In the world of the simulacrum, economically denoted by the superimposed faces of the Jokić family on Rayment's Faucherys (*SM*, pp. 218, 249), authentic history collapses into fabrication. This conundrum, unresolved in *Slow Man*, is its telling component. The idea of 'slowness' then carries with it a cautionary historical principle.

The anxiety over authenticity is also Coetzee's metafictional theme, as he ponders the function of the novel and the novelist. It is here that the impression of 'slowness' can convey the sense of something laboured. When Elizabeth Costello arrives in the novel, a third of the way in, the frame is deliberately broken and the novel changes its tenor. In some respects this is a familiar Coetzean operation, where the realist illusion is laid bare and yet simultaneously relied upon. This unsettling manoeuvre gives rise to some startling effects in the earlier novels – *Life and Times of Michael K* and *Foe* in particular. Here, however, it involves a jolt for the reader, who is no longer able to sustain belief in Coetzee's creation. There is also the nagging feeling that the novel has run out of steam or invention, and that the novelist has recourse to what is, on the face of it, a familiar postmodernist device to keep it afloat. This particular form of self-consciousness – deliberating overtly on the question of artistic inspiration – can be an aggravating form of navel-contemplation, especially when it is the *lack* of inspiration that becomes the focus. Anticipating, or even provoking this thought, Coetzee has Costello reflect to her 'creation' Rayment in these terms, in response to his suggestion that 'taking me up might . . . have been a mistake': 'patience, I tell myself: perhaps there is something yet to be squeezed out of him, like a last drop of juice out of a lemon, or like blood out of a stone. But yes, you may be right, you may indeed be a mistake' (*SM*, pp. 154–5).

Inevitably, this is to provoke an initial sense of impatience in the reader; but it is worth considering what lies behind this dramatic instance of frame-breaking. At the most desultory moment in the novel, Costello summarizes the pervasive unhappiness of all of the characters, and concludes: 'And I am unhappy because nothing is happening. Four people in four corners, moping, like tramps in Beckett, and myself in the middle, wasting time, being wasted by time.' It is the riposte to this from Rayment that is interesting. The narrator reports his internal reflection on being 'signally unmoved' by Costello's 'plea'; and he then retorts 'You do not belong here. This is not your place, not your sphere.' He goes on to make his own plea to this 'outsider': 'Can I not persuade you to leave us alone to work out our salvation in our own way?' (*SM*, p. 141).

Again, this seems, at first glance, a familiar piece of postmodern playfulness, the character in a fiction asserting his independence from his creator. This logical impossibility inevitably underscores the constructed nature of fiction, and the controlling hand of the author. It is a gesture that is customarily held to imply an impulse to relinquish authority, with the author laying bare his or her designs. Because relinquishment has such a particular connotation in Coetzee's work, however, this gesture needs, at the very least, an additional gloss.

Rayment's impulse to resist the authorial design brings us back to the question of place and belonging, since the rejection of Costello is based on his perception of her outsider status. Costello's manipulations of a group of characters, configured to demonstrate the fluidity of national identity under the sign of economic migrancy, is shown to be brittle, as insubstantial as Drago's fake photographs. As a treatment of ethnicity and belonging the novel reveals itself to be a forgery. Partly this has to do with the incapacity of the novel *per se*: as Coetzee has consistently shown, the novel does not lend itself to the treatment of predetermined grand ideas, especially ideas with a political or ideological motivation. In that sense, the novel as a form is just as poorly suited to a treatise on felicitous ethnic hybridity as it is to the presentation of the heroic uprising of the oppressed, where such schema are the expression of political desire.

This does not mean, however, that *Slow Man* cannot contribute usefully to the debate about Australian social hybridity; but it does so with a familiar Coetzean double-move that also casts doubt on the authority of the writer in this connection. And there is also a personal relinquishment of authority for Coetzee in this treatment: if Costello is an outsider to the world of 'her' fiction, Coetzee is an outsider as a new migrant to Australia. His presumption to speak about matters pertaining to Australian ethnicity is tacitly acknowledged in the self-conscious 'stalling' of the novel, so in this respect the mood, timbre and lack of narrative dynamism all point to a personal self-evaluation. At the same time we might wonder if there is, in this, an element of self-projection, especially in the way the novel confines itself to migrant experience. Is Rayment's desire to insert himself in the national culture, through the act of cultural recuperation embodied in the collection of historical photographs, mirrored in Coetzee's effort to write about Australian ethnicity, and to tie in to this topic the question of the authorial role?

The central conundrum of this novel is the accident that befalls Paul Rayment, and which produces the predicament in which he must re-evaluate his inconsequential life, and the single comforting thought that his professional skills will eventually find him a modest role in the national life. It is this presumption that is 'stalled' as much as anything else. This reveals a cautionary note about the willed writing of history, in however small a part. It also, however, represents a return to Coetzee's concern with canonicity at the thematic level: just as *Foe* embodies a postcolonial challenge to – but also an extension of – the canon of the English novel, so does *Slow Man* reveal a related ambivalence. The story of the unfortunate Paul Rayment suggests a fable with a peculiarly Australian dimension, the full significance of migrant experience forcing him to relinquish the notion of stability in which his own niche in the national life might be preserved. The paradox of this, given the acute self-consciousness of the novel, is that it also explodes any presumption on Coetzee's part to have produced an authentic novel of Australian life, even though we may feel he has done so.

Diary of a Bad Year

Diary of a Bad Year (2007) is a still more challenging metafiction, breaking its fragile novelistic frame in extravagant fashion. Part one of the book, 'Strong Opinions', comprises thirty-one mini-essays notionally written by a famous writer 'JC' for a German publisher: he is one of six invited contributors to a book called *Strong Opinions*, and evidently relishes the opportunity for making his pronouncements, especially on weighty global political issues, as one of '*six éminences grises*' (*DBY*, pp. 21, 22). The diary element in part one comprises the thoughts of this JC about the beautiful young woman Anya, whom he encounters in the laundry of his apartment block, develops an infatuation for ('a metaphysical ache', in his words (*DBY*, p. 7)), and subsequently employs as his typist. These reflections are given beneath the mini-essays in a split-page format; and, on page twenty-five, the page splits into three, when Anya's own first-person narrative is added into the mix. Part two of the novel follows a similar format. JC's mini-essays here are more personal and philosophical (he has completed his work on *Strong Opinions*), but they are similarly juxtaposed with two other sections, though here the voice of Alan, Anya's boyfriend, is also heard, through the reported speech of a dinner party at JC's flat.

The immediate challenge presented to the reader of *Diary of a Bad Year* is to assess the portrayal of JC. On the face of it, this is not just a thinly veiled portrait of Coetzee, but an explicit projection of himself: JC's initials (and first name 'John') are Coetzee's, both are white South African writers, newly resident in Australia, and JC's books are also Coetzee's: he mentions 'a collection of essays on censorship' published in the 1990s (*DBY*, p. 22) (which students of Coetzee will identify as *Giving Offense: Essays on Censorship* (1996)), and mentions *Waiting for the Barbarians* as 'my novel' (*DBY*, p. 171). The concern that *Slow Man* raises on an initial reading – that the metafictional operation conceals a degree of creative exhaustion – is also expressly held up for our consideration in *Diary of a Bad Year*. When JC describes the critical opinion of his work that 'at heart he is not a novelist', but rather 'a pedant who dabbles in fiction', he wonders if they are right, and 'whether, all the time I thought I was going about in disguise, I was in fact naked'. This is Coetzee pre-empting the critics; but he runs a considerable risk in evoking the emperor's new clothes. This is compounded when JC describes the fire that drives a creative writer, and observes 'I no longer have it' (*DBY*, pp. 191–2). Yet the terms of the discussion are suddenly changed, when JC reports his distaste for the 'imaginary spectacles' evoked by other novelists: 'I was never much good at evocation of the real' he states, 'and have even less stomach for the task now' (*DBY*, p. 192). What seemed to be an authorial confession, barely disguised, is reoriented towards Coetzee's favoured terrain, the interrogation of realism and the investigation of the limits of fiction.

To the extent that the book invites us to make an equation between Coetzee and JC, we then inevitably ponder how far we should take JC's 'strong opinions' to be those of Coetzee. The condemnation of anti-terrorist legislation in the USA, Britain and Australia is a focus of JC's anger in his essay 'On Terrorism' (*DBY*, p. 22), and this reads like a straightforward piece of political commentary that might well be Coetzee's. Anya's view that JC 'can't get away from Africa' (*DBY*, p. 95) can be plausibly taken as a piece of authorial analysis. And when JC takes the opportunity to reprimand a journalist for misreporting his comments on *Waiting for the Barbarians*, it is possible to miss any discernible fictional element (*DBY*, p. 171). Moments such as these suggest that the structure of *Diary of a Bad Year* affords Coetzee the luxury of a platform to express his own strong opinions, and much of this focuses on the 'war on terror' and the sense of dishonour that descends upon civilian populations where governments perpetrate atrocities in their name.

The book also evokes a strong counter-movement, and this is its crucial aspect. Pursuing the idea of a close correspondence between JC and Coetzee, we are alert for points of divergence. So, when JC appears to have a Nobel Prize scroll, framed, on the wall of his bedroom (*DBY*, p. 47), we spot an instance of self-parody (the pomposity seems absurd), which opens a gap between the two figures. Later we discover JC is 72 (*DBY*, p. 163), and so five or six years older than his creator, one of several clear differences. JC starts to emerge as a development of Elizabeth Costello, an authorial figure that cannot be equated with Coetzee, however tempted we may be to see these creations as the author's mouthpieces at given moments. And then we realize that the invitation to make the comparison is really a device, which serves to open up a debate about the artifice of fiction, and its place in the world of ideas.

A clear indication of the 'fictionality' of the mini-essays in *Diary of a Bad Year* is that they are unlike Coetzee's own essays, which are even in tone, carefully argued, and not the stuff of 'strong opinions'. We are pitched into a debate with JC's opinions, and find ourselves having mixed reactions, especially where rationality and inclination may be at odds. Anya has an important role to play in unsettling the authority of JC's opinions. As his typist, she reveals herself to be more than the bimbo he initially sees in her: she ventures her 'opinion of his opinions', offering what she calls 'a perspective from below', feeling him to be 'out of touch with the modern world' (*DBY*, p. 196). The tempering of his thoughts has issued in what she calls his 'Soft Opinions' (*DBY*, p. 193), and these, presumably, are the mini-essays in part two of the novel.

There are sufficient clues in JC's essays, however, for us to realize that the central experience of the novel is to ponder the difficult relationship between fiction and non-fiction. Arrestingly, JC concludes his essay 'On Terrorism' with a reflection on poetic language, and 'the metaphoric spark', which 'is always one jump ahead of the decoding function, where another, unforeseen reading is always possible' (*DBY*, p. 23). This clear hint about the difficulty of interpretation signals the experimental treatment of ideas with which we are engaged. And when we become attuned to the abrasive nature of this treatment, some of the essays cry out for dissent or debate. A startling instance of this is the argument against literary theory that concludes the essay 'On Al Qaida'. JC summarizes a BBC documentary in which the US administration stood accused of keeping alive 'the myth of Al Qaida as a powerful secret terrorist organization' when it 'has been more or less destroyed'. The programme reported the prosecution of four American Muslims, accused of planning an attack on Disneyland. A home video, presented as evidence of a reconnaissance trip, despite its evidently poor quality, was interpreted as an instance of special cunning: 'the very amateurishness of the video was ground for suspicion, since, where Al Qaida is concerned, nothing is what it seems to be' (*DBY*, pp. 31–2).

This paranoid habit of thinking, suggests JC, has its origins 'in literature classes in the United States of the 1980s and 1990s' where students learned that 'in criticism suspiciousness is the chief virtue':

> From their exposure to literary theory those not-very-bright graduates
> of the academy of the humanities in its postmodernist phase bore away
> a set of analytical instruments which they obscurely sensed could be
> useful outside the classroom, and an intuition that the ability to argue
> that nothing is as it seems to be might get you places.   (*DBY*, p. 33)

Concerns about the educational efficacy of literary theory, and its portable simplifications, are not uncommon; neither is the articulation of such concerns in the pages of a novel. What is noteworthy here, however, is the implication that theory has generated something reactionary, when the usual complaint is that, by encouraging a relative world-view, it has contributed to a form of moral lassitude, and has opened up the spaces in liberal democracies where extremism can flourish. This is a particularly obvious instance of a principle that obtains more subtly throughout the work, where the apparent certainties of an argument are loosened. It is a form of counterpoint in a novel structured carefully to reveal different kinds of counterpoint.

In his essay 'J.S. Bach', JC hints at the inspiration for the principle of counterpoint in the novel. The effects generated through this form of patterning come chiefly from the juxtaposition of the different sections on the page, and can invite a number of interpretive puzzles. One example, chosen at random, is the first page of the essay 'On Al Qaida' referred to above. In the essay section of the page, JC discusses the possibility, apropos of the BBC documentary, that the US administration is deliberately exaggerating the dangers posed by Islamic terrorism. In the middle section of the page, JC reflects on his poor handwriting, and the need to use a Dictaphone as well, for Anya's sake. In the bottom section, Anya's thoughts on her deliberate sexy wiggle are given. Initially, this seems like a bathetic descent from politics, to illness and senility, to the cynical parading of sexuality, the sections linked by the theme of appearance and reality, and the problems of interpretation. Pondering the counterpoint, however, we must wonder whether or not the signs of senility are apparent in the essay, with its pronouncements about 'acts of terrorism that are easy enough to bring off'. And Anya's consciousness of JC's age tempers our reading of her provocativeness, making her seem feisty rather than mindless, on reflection. She reports her response to JC's question, 'where were you born?': 'Why do you want to know? I replied. Am I not blonde-eyed and blue-haired enough for your tastes?' Whether or not we accept this as believable dialogue, the Aryan echo reveals Anya's hidden complexity, as she is able to imply a degree of unconscious racism in his assumption about her, while also hinting, in the deliberate confusion of colours ('blonde-eyed and blue-haired'), that she is too young for him (*DBY*, p. 31).

At first glance, *Diary of a Bad Year* can seem more of a treatise on fiction than a work of fiction in itself. Yet its self-conscious interrogation of modes serves to blur the line between fiction and non-fiction, just as unexpected points of overlap and convergence between the sections on the subdivided pages are discovered. It is another instance of Coetzee pushing at the limits of the novel in a way that makes the authorial persona a central focus. It is, in short, a typically Coetzean work, developing ideas from previous works, and making them fresh, and incorporating a way of wrong-footing the casual reader.

Chapter 5

Reception

Coetzee is one of the most studied contemporary authors, widely taught on undergraduate and postgraduate courses, and his works have been a focus of intense debate for postcolonial critics. This is partly due to the burning importance of the late-colonial situation in South Africa until the final demise of apartheid in 1994, and the instructive position of a white South African writer in relation to that context. But it has also to do with the politically oblique nature of Coetzee's expression, which has tended to divide critics, and to frustrate those looking for a more overtly interventionist form of writing. Increasingly, however, critics have responded favourably to the subtle textual nuances of Coetzee's work. One prominent poststructuralist critic, sensitive to the political potential in Coetzee's literary preoccupations, is Gayatri Spivak, who, writing on *Foe*, finds that novel's metafictional orientation serves to *supplement* rather than oppose more directly interventionist writing on South Africa. ('Theory in the Margin: Coetzee's *Foe* Reading Defoe's *Crusoe/Roxana*', p. 175.) Increasingly, Coetzee's work has provoked elegant and sophisticated work on the theoretical allusiveness of the novels.

The first book devoted to Coetzee was Teresa Dovey's *The Novels of J. M. Coetzee: Lacanian Allegories* (1988). In its application of Lacan, this book was important as the first attempt to read Coetzee through the sophisticated lens of poststructuralist theory; Dovey also established an idea that has become a staple point of debate in Coetzee studies: that the novels can be read as self-referential allegories in which the use of discourse is held up for examination. This book did some important groundwork in Coetzee studies: it sought to identify a kind of hybrid that issues in the work of an academic-as-writer, where literary theory and creative writing inform each other. This has enabled subsequent critics, following Dovey's cue, to suggest that Coetzee's highly self-conscious novels pre-empt his critics. In turn, this establishes the key battleground in Coetzee studies. On the one hand, there are those who believe his work (especially his earlier work) is either complicitous, or weak, in a political sense, an inadequate response to the horrors of apartheid South Africa and its legacy. On the other hand, there are those who have argued, in the spirit of Dovey, that where issues of complicity are treated in Coetzee's work, they are treated self-consciously, as part of the writer's project.

The next two monographs formed a sharp contrast. Dick Penner's *Countries of the Mind: The Fiction of J. M. Coetzee* (1989) was the first study published from the USA, and it lays emphasis on the wider resonance of the novels, beyond the South African context. The title of the book indicates its deliberate attempt to unhook Coetzee's significance from a particular geographical place, and to extract from the novels broader lessons concerning domination and colonialism. Penner also traces the influence of the South African farm novel on Coetzee's work; and, although subsequent critics have not found his book convincing, this has been a recurring topic in Coetzee criticism. Susan VanZanten Gallagher's *A Story of South Africa: J. M. Coetzee's Fiction in Context* (1991) is written from an opposing perspective, as its title suggests. Gallagher considers Coetzee's novels (up to *Age of Iron*) in relation to South African politics, suggesting particular correspondences between the novels and historical events. She shows, for example, how a climate of state repression and torture in the late 1970s, in the aftermath of the Soweto riots of 1976 (and with the mysterious death of Steve Biko in police custody in 1977 as a focal point), appears to have inspired the treatment of torture and repression in *Waiting for the Barbarians*. Gallagher, defending Coetzee from the charge of apolitical withdrawal, finds his work steeped in historical events.

David Attwell's *J. M. Coetzee: South Africa and the Politics of Writing* (1993) was a significant landmark in Coetzee criticism. Between 1989 and 1991 Attwell had collaborated with Coetzee on the collection of essays and interviews published in 1992 as *Doubling the Point*. As editor of that collection he presented a more or less chronological account of Coetzee's development, showing his intellectual allegiances by grouping his critical essays into phases. The essays are punctuated with nine very interesting 'interviews', which were evidently planned and written down as they evolved, and which get to the heart of Coetzee's project as he sees it: in Attwell he evidently found an interviewer he knew and trusted. A crucial point that emerges from the book is that, having turned away from a career in computers, to return to literature as an academic and a novelist, Coetzee feels that his career was governed for fifteen years by a 'formalistic, linguistically based regimen' before he was able to make his 'philosophical engagement with a situation in the world', and to engage with 'the idea of justice' (*DP*, pp. 394–5). *Doubling the Point* now seems especially valuable as a piece of intellectual biography/autobiography.

The following year saw the publication of Attwell's monograph, the first book to embrace convincingly the range of self-reflexive textuality in Coetzee's work, while conveying the clear sense of its rootedness in time and place. It is a landmark piece of criticism in drawing together the tendencies that were beginning to divide Coetzee critics into opposing camps. Attwell presents Coetzee's oeuvre (up to *Age of Iron*) 'as a form of situational metafiction, with a particular relation to the cultural and political discourses of South Africa in the 1970s and 1980s' (p. 3). Attwell is particularly strong on Coetzee's intellectual sources, especially his influences in post-structuralist theory. His analysis of *Life and Times of Michael K* is a good example of how he accounts for these intellectual influences while remaining alert to the presence of history as a shaping influence on the fiction. He shows 'how one might speak of K as the narratological figure of the Der-ridean trace'. Yet the elusive meaning that accompanies Coetzee's evocation of deconstruction in this novel does not, for Attwell, represent a refusal to engage with the political, since Coetzee's reluctance to represent mass resistance or to project a utopian future has very much to do with his ongoing interrogation of positions of authority. Such insights enable us to see the elusive quality of such a novel as an attribute of its political responsibility, rather than a denial of it (pp. 93, 99).

Attwell has floated various terms that might help to categorize Coetzee's work. In one of the interviews in *Doubling the Point*, for example, he suggests that Coetzee might be 'inhabiting a form of late modernism' (*DP*, p. 198). Apropos of *Foe*, Attwell employs the term 'colonial post-colonialism' to describe the 'discursive conditions obtaining in South Africa' to which Coetzee responds (p. 112). But, in the introduction to his book, he argues that 'Coetzee's first six novels constitute a form of postmodern metafiction' (p. 1). These should be seen as overlapping, rather than contradictory pos-itions, contributions to a debate that is becoming more, rather than less complex as fresh criticism appears. Two other monographs are André Viola's *J. M. Coetzee: Romancier Sud-Africain* (published in French, 1999), and my own *J. M. Coetzee* (1997), in the series 'Cambridge Studies in African and Caribbean Literature', which covers the first half of Coetzee's career (from the current historical vantage point), up to *The Master of Petersburg*.

An early collection of critical essays emerged from a special issue of *The South Atlantic Quarterly* (1994) edited by Michael Valdez Moses, and also published in book form as *The Writings of J. M. Coetzee*. Several of the (now) central points of debate in Coetzee studies were covered: ethics and politics, the pastoral mode, Coetzee's influences, silence and oppression. By this time, Coetzee's work was becoming increasingly prominent in academic study, and, as we have seen, two opposing – even polarized – critical perspectives emerged. On the one hand there were those critics who thought his works failed to live up to the demands of political representation and historical fidelity; and on the other there were those critics, reading from a post-structuralist perspective, who found his books much richer.

These contrasting views are clearly evident in an important collection of essays edited by Graham Huggan and Stephen Watson, *Critical Perspectives on J. M. Coetzee* (1996). Huggan and Watson summarize Coetzee's work as possessing 'a disquieting vision, with those distinctly apocalyptic, even nihilistic overtones we usually take to be characteristic of the era of international modernism' (p. 5). An important early essay reprinted in this collection, also troubled by the political implications of Coetzee's style, is Peter Knox-Shaw's '*Dusklands*: A Metaphysics of Violence'. Knox-Shaw finds the treatment of colonial violence in *Dusklands* to be imprisoning, the novel betraying 'an art that can only re-enact'. The ironic undercutting of the perpetrators of colonial projects he feels to be inadequate for the treatment of the brutality depicted in the novel (p. 114).

This book contains some of the most telling critiques of Coetzee, including Stephen Watson's essay 'Colonialism and the Novels of J. M. Coetzee', originally published in *Research in African Literatures*, in which Watson considers in detail the complaint that Coetzee's recourse to mythical/archetypal features amounts to an evasion of history. Watson puts an alternative view, arguing that the novels (up to *Age of Iron*) are grounded in history in the way they provide 'insight into the colonising mind, as well as the dissenting colonising mind' (p. 36). But the essay registers very powerfully the suggestion that, at the heart of Coetzee's novels, there is 'little more than an artfully constructed void', the core of the work lying 'outside the works', in the history to which they 'barely allude' (p. 22).

Still more challenging to Coetzee's defenders is Benita Parry's essay in the same collection. One of the premises of Coetzee's fiction seems to be a reluctance to enact the dominion of canonical literary power; indeed, looking favourably upon Coetzee's work, critics find an earnest effort to lay bare or deconstruct whatever imperial power might reside in the literary. And, to this impulse, critics frequently relate Coetzee's refusal to 'speak for' the colonized or marginalized other in his works. In her essay 'Speech and Silence in the Fictions of J. M. Coetzee', Parry acknowledges these narrative strategies, but puts forward the 'polemical proposition' that such strategies are flawed: his fictions may well disrupt 'colonialist modes'; yet, she argues, 'the social authority on which their rhetoric relies and which they exert is grounded in the cognitive systems of the West'. More problematic is the refusal to speak for the other, because 'the consequence of writing the silence attributed to the subjugated as a liberation from the constraints of sub-jectivity ... can be read as re-enacting the received disposal of narrative authority' (pp. 39–40). In this view, Coetzee's novels re-inscribe oppression in the very act of resisting it, because of the tradition from which they cannot extricate themselves. Parry's essay reaches a nuanced view on this difficult double bind; but it is the imprisoning aspect of her polemical proposition that resonates.

Also in the Huggan and Watson collection is Derek Attridge's important essay 'Oppressive Silence: J. M. Coetzee's *Foe* and the Politics of Canonisation'. Attridge reads Coetzee's engagement with the inscription of literary power very differently from Benita Parry, demonstrating how Coetzee's literary allusiveness produces a different kind of ambivalence, on the one hand serving to expose 'the ideological basis of canonisation', while also revealing 'its own relation to the existing canon' (p. 171). Attridge's 'utopian' and speculative conclusion is that if texts like Coetzee's – texts that 'question the very processes of canonicity' – are admitted to the canon, we may witness a transformation of the 'ideology and the institutions from which the canon derives its power, so that new ... ways of finding a voice, and new ways of hearing such voices, come into being' (p. 186). Another critic represented in this collection who is sensitive to Coetzee's scrupulous treatment of the other is Michael Marais. Marais has written several note-worthy essays, inspired by Levinas, on Coetzee's ongoing preoccupation with ethics and otherness (see the section on 'Further reading').

Another essay collection appeared in 1998, edited by Sue Kossew: *Critical Essays on J. M. Coetzee*. Published in the G. K. Hall series 'Critical Essays on World Literature', the brief for this collection was chiefly to reprint and bring to the attention of a wider audience significant essays from more obscure scholarly publications. Essays by several of the prominent Coetzee critics, including Dovey, Attwell, Attridge and Marais, were reprinted. Also included is a revised version of an essay by Brian Macaskill, 'Charting J. M. Coetzee's Middle Voice: *In the Heart of the Country*', originally pub-lished in *Contemporary Literature*. This is a noteworthy contribution to the discussion of Coetzee's self-consciousness, and to how he deploys narrative strategies to position himself against the cultural politics that dominated ideas about South African writing in the first part of his career.

Also included in Kossew's collection is a specially commissioned essay by Bill Ashcroft – 'Irony, Allegory and Empire: *Waiting for the Barbarians* and *In the Heart of the Country*' – a contribution to the seminal topic of post-colonial allegory, seminal for postcolonial studies generally, and for an evaluation of Coetzee in particular. The best-known reprinted piece in the collection, however, is Nadine Gordimer's 'The Idea of Gardening', her review of *Life and Times of Michael K.* This important review, which is discussed in chapter 3 above, was one of those documents that helped consolidate an expectation of realist intervention in the South African writer: Gordimer finds Coetzee's allegorical mode unfit for the task in hand. She does, however, in a rather bemused reflection on the novel's ecological theme, point the way for postcolonial ecocritics with an interest in Coetzee. A critic who might be said to have pioneered this kind of approach is Derek Wright. (See his essay 'Black Earth, White Myth: Coetzee's *Michael K*'.)

In her book *Pen and Power: A Post-Colonial Reading of J. M. Coetzee and André Brink* (1996), Kossew works with a productive series of comparisons between Coetzee and Brink. She keeps in view the key differences between Coetzee's postmodernism and Brink's social realism; but she also subjects those categories to extended scrutiny, showing them to be porous. Through this process, Coetzee is shown to be more politically engaged (and Brink more alert to the implications of language and textuality) than is sometimes assumed. Kossew offers an informed understanding of Coetzee's contribution to postcolonial writing, arguing that his significance is becoming clearer in the post-apartheid era.

It is something of a paradox that Coetzee's international reputation increased exponentially with the publication of *Disgrace*. This was the novel that was the first to secure a second Booker win for a previously successful author; and it must have been a significant factor in the award of the Nobel Prize a few years later. This was a commercially successful novel, perhaps because it was written ostensibly in a realist mode. This book, then, seemingly unrepresentative of Coetzee's oeuvre, was the one that sealed his international reputation. The most surprising aspect of this is that *Disgrace* also seemed to advance the estimation of Coetzee amongst academics. A special issue of *Scrutiny2* was devoted to *Disgrace*, with an editorial that caught the mood: 'this issue of *Scrutiny2* bears witness to an extraordinary phenomenon – "a spontaneous overflow of powerful feelings" one might say, following Wordsworth – upon the subject of J. M. Coetzee's novel, *Disgrace*' (p. 3). In the same year a special issue of *Interventions* devoted to *Disgrace* appeared, edited by Derek Attridge and Peter D. McDonald.

Here, however, we might note a significant divergence between the popular international interest in *Disgrace*, which may suggest a recognition of Coetzee's most direct engagement with South African society, and the emphases of that 'spontaneous overflow' amongst academics, who argued about the political dimension of the novel, but who also placed emphasis on the ethical and aesthetic aspects of the book. Ultimately, it is this duality that gives *Disgrace* its true significance. In Coetzee studies, this provided a focus for beginning to bring together ethical and political readings.

Another aspect of the appeal of *Disgrace* amongst academics, and the phase of Coetzee's writing to which it belongs, is the interrogation of the role of the intellectual. A collection of essays that places emphasis on this phase, and which examines Coetzee's treatment of intellectual work, is *J. M. Coetzee and the Idea of the Public Intellectual* (2006), edited by Jane Poyner. With a focus on *Disgrace*, *The Lives of Animals* and *Elizabeth Costello*, the collection, which grew out of an international conference on Coetzee at the University of Warwick, brings together ethical and political concerns in new ways that are appropriate to Coetzee's post-apartheid writing. It includes essays by Derek Attridge, David Attwell, Michael Bell, Sam Durrant, Lucy Graham and Rosemary Jolly, amongst others. Violence (especially against women) is a recurring topic in this collection; but Coetzee's representation of violence is not confined to his more recent works. (Rosemary Jolly's earlier consideration of the forms of violence in *Dusklands* and *Waiting for the Barbarians* is an important treatment of the topic. See *Colonization, Violence, and Narration in White South African Writing* (1996).)

Some of the most arresting passages in Coetzee's more recent work have involved animals. One such is the much-discussed episode in *Disgrace*, discussed in the previous chapter, in which we are made privy to Lurie's rationalization for taking responsibility for incinerating the dogs' corpses. In his book *The Philosopher's Dog*, moral philosopher Raimond Gaita picks up on the apparent irrationality of worrying about the 'honour' of the dead dogs; but he explains that he quotes Coetzee in the hope that such rationalists 'might find him persuasive even if they are not in the end persuaded', and because he wants 'to reflect on what it means to be rightly persuaded by a writer of such grace and power' (p. 93). Given that the question of literary alterity has become central to Coetzee studies, this approach to it, from the perspective of moral philosophy, is worthy of attention.

Another passage involving animals that, quite self-consciously, draws attention to itself as difficult to interpret (and so serves to highlight for us the difficulty of interpretation more generally) is the substance of Elizabeth Costello's second petition 'at the gate'. This statement of belief presents a childhood memory of rural Victoria, on the river Dulgannon, and the sight of thousands of little frogs entombed in sun-baked mud, revived by seasonal rains. Costello asserts that she believes in the frogs, and most especially because of the frogs' indifference to her belief. In an excellent review of the novel, James Wood suggests that this is 'the moment at which this highly religious book finally declares itself – but only to appropriate religion in a pagan turn . . . To enter the frog's life is like entering a fictional character's life. And this is a kind of religion, akin to the worship of a God who gives us nothing back' ('A Frog's Life', p. 16). This is a valuable piece that highlights the importance of Coetzee's appropriation of religious motifs and ideas for his own creative purposes – as in this metafictional deliberation about the frogs.

The most significant book on Coetzee to date is Derek Attridge's *J. M. Coetzee and the Ethics of Reading: Literature in the Event* (2004), a book that gathers together Attridge's essays on Coetzee, in the context of an over-arching argument that illustrates the principles of reading established in Attridge's *The Singularity of Literature* (2004). Indeed, Attridge has presented the two books as complementary, since Coetzee's oeuvre 'explores and exemplifies with particular intensity and urgency' the issues addressed in the theoretical book (*Singularity*, p. xii).

In *The Singularity of Literature* Attridge seeks to oppose 'an increasingly instrumental approach to literature' in university life, a trend that he presents as 'part of a more general, globally experienced increase in the weight given to the values of the market-place, to the success ethic, to productivity as a measure of worth' (p. 9). By contrast, responsive and creative reading requires that the reader resists the temptation to read a literary work according to a predetermined set of expectations. Such reading 'involves a suspension of habits, a willingness to rethink old positions in order to apprehend the work's inaugural power' (p. 80).

Such an open and creative approach to reading invokes an ethical responsibility – openness to the otherness and inventiveness of the text – that is paralleled in the ethics of literature, or the ethical sense that literature can generate. For Attridge, 'to read a work responsibly . . . is to read it without placing over it a grid of possible uses, as historical evidence, moral lesson, path to truth, political inspiration, or personal encouragement . . . It is to trust in the unpredictability of reading, its openness to the future' (pp. 129–30).

In *J. M. Coetzee and the Ethics of Reading*, Attridge demonstrates, with reference to Coetzee, how his theory of responsible reading is based on an understanding of 'the literary work as an event' in which the reader 'brings the work into being, differently each time, in a singular performance of the work' (p. 9). This is not to deny that historical and contextual forces operate on authors and readers, helping to shape writing and understanding; but it reinstates the idea of the literary effect, and gives due place to the unpre-dictability and mutability of literary language. An especially noteworthy section of the book is the second chapter, 'Against Allegory', which focuses on *Waiting for the Barbarians* and *Life and Times of Michael K.* Attridge argues that a straightforward allegorical reading, in which characters and events are revealed to have correspondences in the real world, defeats a 'literary reading' in which the text 'comes into being only in the process of understanding and responding' (p. 39). Attridge is conscious, however, that some novels (like Coetzee's) seem partially to invite us to allegorize, so that 'part of the literary experience may be *the event of the allegorising reading*'. This means that 'allegory may . . . be *staged* in literature' (p. 61).

Attridge's insistence on 'the contingent, the processual, the provisional' in a form of reading 'that keeps moral questions alive' is plainly incompatible with that form of instrumental reading that would appropriate Coetzee as a 'South African novelist', judged in terms of the 'adequacy' of his responses to changing political circumstances (p. 54). Yet, for some critics this will be to avoid the centrality of the South African context to Coetzee's life and works. More problematic is the apparently close fit between Attridge's theory of responsible reading – and the global context to which it responds – and Coetzee's own implied views on that context, and on the function of literature. Attridge's opposition to a static form of 'allegorizing reading', especially that kind of reading which results from 'the urge to apply pre-existing norms and to make fixed moral judgments', is clearly of a piece with his distrust of a regulated and goal-driven society (p. 54). And he is able to find very similar ideas in Coetzee's own work – for example, in the 'satiric portrayal' in *Disgrace* of 'reductive, management-driven methods' in university life (*Singularity*, p. 6).

Here it is tempting to invoke, once more, Coetzee's own concern about the nature of criticism: 'what can it ever be, but either a betrayal (the usual case) or an overpowering (the rarer case) of its object? How often is there an equal marriage?' (*DP*, p. 61). Like the colonizer, armed with his own inflexible codes for understanding the world, the reader must baulk at his or her own inclination to order, simplify, explain, in the face of the alterity of the text. Here we may well be justified in making a clear connection between recent enthusiasm for narrative ethics/the ethics of reading, and the resisting Coetzee text. This is a clear invitation to distrust blunt 'allegorical' readings in the way that Attridge does.

Indeed, Attridge's theory of reading is the response of a sophisticated critic, agreeing with Coetzee's insistence on the autonomy of the writer and the novel, especially the felt need to establish a position of 'rivalry' with history, when the only other option seems to be 'supplementarity' ('The Novel Today'). Attridge's construction of the critical reading as an ethical event finds its perfect exemplar in Coetzee, whose novels seem, in a way, to agitate for precisely the critical school that Attridge advocates. Is this the 'equal marriage' between critic and work that Coetzee implies is virtually impossible – or something close to it? It would appear to be so; and one is left with nothing but admiration for Attridge in having achieved this hard-won correspondence, over a period of years reading and reflecting on the various contours of Coetzee's career. Yet we must also wonder whether or not such an equal marriage is desirable. For many academic literary critics this will surely indicate a loss of proper critical distance.

This is not a conundrum that can be resolved here, though it will doubtless be a running theme in Coetzee studies as Attridge's fine book continues to exert its influence. There are, however, two things that are worth observing. First, the academic impulse to reject the close fit between a critic and a writer may be revealing about its own position, an indication of the instrumental professionalism that Attridge and Coetzee are both at pains to resist. Second, the idea of this equal marriage, when applied to a single author and the ideas about writing and criticism his fictional works seem to stimulate, can operate at only a very generalized level. The connection may become more or less visible in response to the shifting emphases in successive works.

One of the issues that is potentially problematic in Attridge's approach, and which will certainly rankle with politically minded critics, is the idea of being open to the alterity of a text, wherever that may lead. Such openness requires in the reader a willingness 'to take on trust' that a work 'has something valuable to say when it appears obscure or objectionable, at least until several readings ... make an informed and just response possible' (*Singularity*, p. 125). It is easy to see why some postcolonial critics will consider this to be too leisurely a mode of critical evaluation. Yet it is a principle explored in Coetzee's novels, most notably in *The Master of Petersburg*, where the idea of writing as a form of personal betrayal emerges as one consequence of opening oneself fully to the other. This problematic aspect of a difficult novel seems deliberately to sully any claim that ethical responsibility resides, inherently, in literary creativity. Mention should be made here of Stephen Watson's perceptive essay, 'The Writer and the Devil', which brings out very fully the uncomfortable ambivalence of Coetzee's novel, with regard to the dilemma of the writer.

There is also, in Attridge's theory of responsible reading, the possibility of a form of instrumentality in the uses to which literature is put; and this reveals a slight, but important gap between the critic and the writer, which unsettles the seemingly cosy relationship, and re-establishes a significant degree of autonomy. This qualified position of independence is what necessarily follows from Attridge's insistence that the critical reader must 'trust in the unpredictability of reading, its openness to the future'. Attridge goes on to say: 'from this reading, of course, a responsible instrumentality may follow, perhaps one with modified methods or goals' (*Singularity*, p. 130).

That idea of 'responsible instrumentality' assigns a place for the critic's own intellectual context; and, in doing so, it opens up the possibility of some kind of rapprochement between those critics, like Attridge, who prioritize the ethical dimension of Coetzee's work, and those who feel that particular contextual resonances determine the reception of his work. In debating the applicability of Attridge, that is to say, Coetzee critics may come to bridge the polarized positions that have been evident in some of the critical literature. Laura Wright's book, *Writing 'Out of All the Camps': J. M. Coetzee's Narratives of Displacement* (2006) is a 'post-Attridge' work that draws together the ethical and the political, and builds intelligently on previous Coetzee criticism. Wright responds to previous debates about allegory in Coetzee's work – and especially Attridge's observations about Coetzee's self-conscious use of allegory against itself – in order to define the imaginative realm of the novels in different terms, as 'performative fables'. The book can be seen as an instance of postcolonial ecocriticism, a hybrid form of literary theory that is becoming increasingly important. Recognizing the importance of animals in Coetzee's work, Wright reads 'Coetzee's narratives as performative examinations of the nature of imagined identification with the other', which here includes animals as well as marginalized or oppressed human figures.

This survey of Coetzee criticism is intended merely to identify important trends and to highlight significant instances that have had, or are likely to have, an enduring impact on Coetzee studies. But it is a rapidly expanding field of criticism – there are several more books (including essay collections) in press as I write – and one that is bound to become increasingly complex.

I shall conclude this survey by quoting from a little-known short essay by Coetzee on the topic of 'thematic criticism', because it encapsulates the dilemmas that face all critics of Coetzee. The very idea of 'thematic criticism', understood as the identification of 'themes' in a literary work, would seem to be precisely the kind of reductive criticism – the unresponsive rewriting of a text in other words – that students of Coetzee must be wary of, even while recognizing that this pitfall may inevitably catch out all who are involved in the act of criticism. Something of this double bind is conveyed in Coetzee's short piece 'Thematizing', from the writer's perspective. Pondering how themes enter the writing process, Coetzee writes of 'a certain back-and-forth motion'. First, as a writer, 'you give yourself to (or throw yourself into) the writing'; and 'then you step back and ask yourself where you are, whether you really want to be there'. The process of taking stock – 'interrogation', Coetzee calls it – 'entails conceptualising, and specifically thematizing, what you have written (or what has been written out of you)'.

In his own writing experience, Coetzee reveals that this motion is 'regular and habitual'. Crucially, he states:

> In my account, it is not the theme that counts but thematizing. What themes emerge in the process are heuristic, provisional, and in that sense insignificant. The reasoning imagination thinks in themes because those are the only means it has; but the means are not the ends. ('Thematizing', p. 289)

What is true of the creative process must be true of the critical process in a related way: attempting to make provisional sense of a rich and complex writer like Coetzee in a critical account (and especially an introductory account) must involve getting to grips with this thematizing, and the identification of themes, in the hope that these may be useful signposts for the reader's own more significant and enriching encounter with the irreducible literary works themselves.

Further reading

Primary texts

Dusklands. Johannesburg: Ravan Press, 1974; Harmondsworth: Penguin, 1983.
In the Heart of the Country. London: Secker and Warburg, 1977;
      Harmondsworth: Penguin, 1982.
Waiting for the Barbarians. London: Secker and Warburg, 1980;
      Harmondsworth: Penguin, 1982.
Life and Times of Michael K. London: Secker and Warburg, 1983;
      Harmondsworth: Penguin, 1985.
Foe. London: Secker and Warburg, 1986; Harmondsworth: Penguin, 1987.
White Writing: On the Culture of Letters in South Africa. New Haven: Yale
      University Press, 1988.
'The Novel Today', *Upstream*, 6 (1988), 1, pp. 2–5.
Age of Iron. London: Secker and Warburg, 1990; Harmondsworth: Penguin, 1991.
'Breyten Breytenbach and the Censor' (1991), in *De-Scribing Empire:*
      Postcolonialism and Textuality, eds. Chris Tiffin and Alan Lawson.
      London: Routledge, 1994, pp. 86–97.
Doubling the Point: Essays and Interviews, ed. David Attwell. Cambridge, MA.:
      Harvard University Press, 1992.
'Thematizing', in *The Return of Thematic Criticism*, ed. Werner Sollors.
      Cambridge MA.: Harvard University Press, 1993, p. 289.
The Master of Petersburg. London: Secker and Warburg, 1994.
'Meat Country', in *Granta*, 52 (Winter 1995), pp. 41–52.
Giving Offense: Essays on Censorship. Chicago: University of Chicago Press, 1996.
Boyhood: Scenes From Provincial Life. London: Secker and Warburg, 1997.
The Lives of Animals, ed. Amy Gutman. Princeton NJ: Princeton University
      Press, 1999.
Disgrace. London: Secker and Warburg, 1999.
Stranger Shores: Essays 1986–1999. London: Secker and Warburg, 2001.
Youth. London: Secker and Warburg, 2002.
Slow Man. London: Secker and Warburg, 2005.
Inner Workings: Literary Essays 2000–2005, Introduction by Derek Attridge.
      London: Harvill Secker, 2007.
Diary of a Bad Year. London: Harvill Secker, 2007.

Secondary texts

Ashcroft, Bill, 'Irony, Allegory and Empire: *Waiting for the Barbarians* and *In the Heart of the Country*', in *Critical Essays on J. M. Coetzee*, ed. Sue Kossew, pp. 100–16.

A contribution to the seminal topic of postcolonial allegory – seminal for postcolonial studies generally, and for an evaluation of Coetzee in particular.

Attridge, Derek, 'Oppressive Silence: J. M. Coetzee's *Foe* and the Politics of Canonisation', in *Critical Perspectives on J. M. Coetzee*, eds. Graham Huggan and Stephen Watson, pp. 168–90.

Demonstrates the ambivalence of Coetzee's literary allusiveness, which exposes 'the ideological basis of canonisation', while also revealing Coetzee's own stake in 'the existing canon', and in transforming it.

The Singularity of Literature. London: Routledge, 2004.

Opposing 'an increasingly instrumental approach to literature' in university life, Attridge advocates a form of responsive and creative reading which requires that the reader resists the temptation to read a literary work according to a predetermined set of expectations. The companion volume to *J. M. Coetzee and the Ethics of Reading*.

J. M. Coetzee and the Ethics of Reading: Literature in the Event. Chicago: University of Chicago Press, 2004.

A major work on Coetzee, and the most significant book to date. Attridge gathers together various essays in the context of an over-arching argument that illustrates the principles of reading established in *The Singularity of Literature*.

Attridge, Derek, and Peter McDonald, eds., 'J. M. Coetzee's *Disgrace*', special issue, *Interventions: International Journal of Postcolonial Studies*, 4 (2002), 3.

A journal special issue devoted to *Disgrace*.

Attwell, David, *J. M. Coetzee: South Africa and the Politics of Writing.* Berkeley: University of California Press, 1993.

The first book to embrace convincingly the range of self-reflexive textuality in Coetzee's work, while conveying the clear sense of its rootedness in time and place.

Bakhtin, Mikhail, *Problems of Dostoevsky's Poetics*, trans. Caryl Emerson. Manchester: Manchester University Press, 1984.

Contains the analysis of Dostoevsky's *Demons* that has had an influential bearing on Coetzee's developing ideas about confession.

Bhabha, Homi, *The Location of Culture.* London: Routledge, 1994.

Proposes the idea of a 'postcolonial time-lag' that allows the discourses of modernity to be addressed from a postcolonial perspective. There may be a suggestive way of thinking about Coetzee's position 'between' modernism and postmodernism.

Dovey, Teresa, *The Novels of J. M. Coetzee: Lacanian Allegories.* Craighall: Donker, 1988.
>   The first book on Coetzee. A Lacanian reading, and so the first attempt at a sustained reading through the lens of poststructuralist theory.
During, Simon, 'Postmodernism or Post-colonialism Today', *Textual Practice,* 1 (1987), 1, pp. 32–47; extract printed in *The Post-colonial Studies Reader,* eds. Bill Ashcroft, Gareth Griffiths and Helen Tiffin. London: Routledge, 1995, pp. 125–9.
>   Contains a useful distinction that might help locate Coetzee's historical position in the apartheid years. During distinguishes between the 'post-colonized', those who identify with the culture overlaid by imperialism, and by the language of the colonizer on the one hand; and the 'post-colonizers', those who are embroiled in the culture and language of colonialism, even while they reject imperialism, on the other.
Gaita, Raimond, *The Philosopher's Dog.* London: Routledge, 2003.
>   Moral philosopher Raimond Gaita's book contains a noteworthy deliberation on the 'honour' of the dead dogs in *Disgrace.*
Gallagher, Susan VanZanten, *A Story of South Africa: J. M. Coetzee's Fiction in Context.* Cambridge, MA.: Harvard University Press, 1991.
>   Considers the novels (up to *Age of Iron*) in relation to South African politics, suggesting particular correspondences with historical events.
Goddard, Kevin, and John Read, *J. M. Coetzee: A Bibliography.* Grahamstown: NELM, 1990.
>   A useful bibliographical resource.
Gordimer, Nadine, 'The Idea of Gardening', *New York Review of Books,* 2 January 1984, pp. 3–6.
>   An important review, which helped consolidate an expectation of realist intervention in the South African writer: Gordimer finds Coetzee's allegorical mode unfit for the task in hand.
Head, Dominic, *J. M. Coetzee.* Cambridge: Cambridge University Press, 1997.
>   Written for the series 'Cambridge Studies in African and Caribbean Literature'. Covers the first half of Coetzee's career, up to *The Master of Petersburg.*
Hegel, G. W. F., *Phenomenology of Spirit,* trans. A. V. Miller. Oxford: Oxford University Press, 1977.
>   The source of Hegel's work on the master/slave, or lord/bondsman dialectic that has influenced Coetzee, most notably in *In the Heart of the Country.*
Huggan, Graham, and Stephen Watson, eds. *Critical Perspectives on J. M. Coetzee.* London: Macmillan, 1996.
>   An important collection of essays in which the two opposing views of Coetzee were represented: accounts in which Coetzee fails to live up to the demands of political representation and historical fidelity are balanced by post-structuralist readings which present his work as much richer.

Jameson, Fredric, *Postmodernism, or, the Cultural Logic of Late Capitalism*. London: Verso, 1991.
> Seminal work on postmodernism, which includes an account of how, in postmodernist expression, allegory becomes highly self-conscious, a mode that advances a radical investigation of its own grounding. This is the theoretical context in which Coetzee's use of allegory must be considered.

Jolly, Rosemary Jane, *Colonization, Violence, and Narration in White South African Writing: André Brink, Breyten Breytenbach, and J. M. Coetzee*. Athens: Ohio University Press, 1996.
> Contains an important treatment of the forms of violence in *Dusklands* and *Waiting for the Barbarians*.

Knox-Shaw, Peter, '*Dusklands*: A Metaphysics of Violence', *Commonwealth Novel in English*, 2 (1983), 1, pp. 65–81, reprinted in Huggan and Watson, eds., *Critical Perspectives on J. M. Coetzee*, pp. 107–19.
> Knox-Shaw finds the treatment of colonial violence in *Dusklands* to be imprisoning.

Kossew, Sue, ed. *Critical Essays on J. M. Coetzee*. New York: G. K. Hall, 1998.
> Reprints significant essays from more obscure scholarly publications. Features several of the prominent Coetzee critics, including Dovey, Attwell, Attridge and Marais.

Kossew, Sue, *Pen and Power: A Post-Colonial Reading of J. M. Coetzee and André Brink*. Amsterdam: Rodopi, 1996.
> Kossew works with a productive series of comparisons between Coetzee and Brink, enriching and complicating the contrast between Coetzee's postmodernism and Brink's social realism.

Macaskill, Brian, 'Charting J. M. Coetzee's Middle Voice', in *Critical Essays on J. M. Coetzee*, ed. Sue Kossew, pp. 66–83.
> Shows how Coetzee deploys narrative strategies to position himself against the cultural politics that dominated ideas about South African writing in the first part of his career.

Marais, Michael, 'Languages of Power: A Story of Reading Coetzee's *Michael K/Michael K*', *English in Africa*, 16 (1989), 2, pp. 31–48.
> A critic who has been consistently sensitive to Coetzee's scrupulous treatment of the other.

'Little Enough, Less Than Little: Nothing': Ethics, Engagement, and Change in the Fiction of J. M. Coetzee', *Modern Fiction Studies*, 46 (2000), 1, pp. 159–82.
> One example of a series of noteworthy essays by Marais, inspired by Levinas, on Coetzee's ongoing preoccupation with ethics and otherness.

Moses, Michael Valdez, 'The Mark of Empire: Writing, History, and Torture in Coetzee's *Waiting for the Barbarians*', *Kenyon Review*, 15 (1993), 1, pp. 115–27.
> Important essay on *Waiting for the Barbarians* concerning Coetzee's sources in Kafka and Foucault.

ed., 'The Writings of J. M. Coetzee', special issue, *South Atlantic Quarterly*, 93 (1994), 1.

In this journal special issue, also published in book form, several of the (now) central points of debate in Coetzee studies are covered: ethics and politics, the pastoral mode, Coetzee's influences, silence and oppression.

Parry, Benita, 'Speech and Silence in the Fictions of J. M. Coetzee', in *Critical Perspectives on J. M. Coetzee*, eds. Graham Huggan and Stephen Watson, pp. 37–65.

Considers the proposition that Coetzee's novels re-inscribe oppression in the very act of resisting it, because of the tradition from which they cannot extricate themselves.

Penner, Dick, *Countries of the Mind: The Fiction of J. M. Coetzee*. Westport: Greenwood Press, 1989.

The first book-length study published from the USA. It lays emphasis on the wider resonance of the novels, beyond the South African context.

Poyner, Jane, ed., *J. M. Coetzee and the Idea of the Public Intellectual*. Athens: Ohio University Press, 2006.

A collection of essays that places emphasis on the role of the intellectual, with a focus on *Disgrace*, *The Lives of Animals*, and *Elizabeth Costello*,

Slemon, Stephen, 'Post-Colonial Allegory and the Transformation of History', *Journal of Commonwealth Literature*, 23 (1988), 1, pp. 157–68.

An important essay that can be used to help map Coetzee's contribution to postcolonial allegory. In Slemon's account, postcolonial allegory cultivates historical revisionism, since images of received history are alluded to through a process of allegorical correspondence, engaging the reader in a dialectic of discourses.

Spivak, Gayatri, 'Theory in the Margin: Coetzee's *Foe* Reading Defoe's *Crusoe/Roxana*', in *The Consequences of Theory*, eds. Jonathan Arac and Barbara Johnson. Baltimore: Johns Hopkins University Press, 1991, pp. 154–80.

An important intervention by a leading poststructuralist, sensitive to Coetzee's political potential.

Symposium on *Disgrace*, *Scrutiny2*, 7 (2002), 1.

Another journal special issue, devoted to *Disgrace*.

Tiffin, Helen, 'Post-Colonial Literatures and Counter-Discourse', *Kunapipi*, 9 (1987), 3, pp. 17–34.

Tiffin defines that branch of postcolonial culture where 'decolonization is process, not arrival'. In such writing European and local discourses are made to interact, in a dialectical relationship where European discourses are very much present, even while they are partly subverted or dismantled. This idea of 'process, not arrival' has a direct bearing on Coetzee's earlier work.

Viola, André, *J. M. Coetzee: Romancier Sud-Africain*. Paris: Harmattan, 1999.

Monograph published in French.

Watson, Stephen, 'Colonialism and the Novels of J. M. Coetzee', *Research in African Literatures*, 17 (1986), 3, pp. 370–92; reprinted in *Critical Perspectives on J. M. Coetzee*, eds. Huggan and Watson, pp. 13–36. Considers in detail the complaint that Coetzee's recourse to mythical/ archetypal features amounts to an evasion of history. 'The Writer and the Devil: J. M. Coetzee's *The Master of Petersburg*', *New Contrast* 22 (1994), 4, pp. 47–61. Watson brings out very fully the uncomfortable ambivalence of Coetzee's novel, with regard to the dilemma of the writer.

Watt, Ian, *The Rise of the Novel: Studies in Defoe, Richardson and Fielding.* 1957; reprinted, Harmondsworth: Penguin, 1981.
The classic account of the rise of the English novel, to which Coetzee writes back in *Foe*.

Wood, James. 'A Frog's Life', review of *Elizabeth Costello, London Review of Books*, 23 October 2003, 25:20, pp. 15–16.
A valuable review that highlights an instance of Coetzee's appropriation of religious motifs and ideas for his own creative purposes.

Wright, Derek, 'Black Earth, White Myth: Coetzee's *Michael K*', *Modern Fiction Studies*, 38 (1992), 2, pp. 435–44.
A pioneering work of postcolonial ecocriticism.

Wright, Laura, *Writing 'Out of All the Camps': J. M. Coetzee's Narratives of Displacement.* London: Routledge, 2006.
A book that draws together ethical and political arguments. To the extent that Wright recognizes the importance of animals in Coetzee's work, this is an instance of postcolonial ecocriticism.

Yeoh, Gilbert, 'J. M. Coetzee and Samuel Beckett: Nothingness, Minimalism and Indeterminacy', *ARIEL*, 31 (2000), 4, pp. 117–37.
Shows how Coetzee uses certain strategies borrowed from Beckett to address his own personal and historical circumstances. Yeoh thus contributes to the critical view that places great weight on Coetzee's modernist precursors.

Index

The Cambridge Introduction to . . .

AUTHORS

TOPICS